A Time to Remember

Cabra and its People

By
Martin Coffey B.A.

ISBN: 978-1-905451-01-6

A CIP catalogue for this book is available from the National Library.

This book was published in cooperation with
Choice Publishing & Book Services Ltd, Ireland
Tel: 041 9841551 Email: info@choicepublishing.ie
www.choicepublishing.ie

Dedication

This book is dedicated to my parents Bernard and Mary Coffey and to the memory of my younger brother Joe. It is also dedicated to all those people from the Cabra area who deserve to be remembered for the great legacy that they have left behind.

I would like to thank the following people for their support, most of whom have had some input or influence on me during the writing of this book either through lending photographs, sharing stories or words of encouragement.

The Coffey Family, Mary Renehan, my children and grandchildren, , Gracie and Maggie Doyle, Angela Kane, Barney Mulhall, the Burke Family from Broombridge Road, Gerry Walsh KSG, Very Rev. Fr. Ivan Tonge P.P., Larry Maher, The Educational Company of Ireland, Choice Publishing and Book Services Ltd, Eugene Rooney from Annamoe, Shay Jordan from Annamoe, Liam O'Kelly Killala Road, The O'Neill/Hickey Family Carnlough Road, James Rogers Killala Road, Deirdre Price and family Carnlough Road, Tony Dunne Family Cabra Road, Mary Brogan, Willie Lynch New Jersey/Carnlough Road, Martin & Eileen Branagan Carnlough Road, Michael Hayes Killala Road, the Mitchell family Killala Road, George Marshall, Dennis Doyle, Charlie Brogan Killala Road, Mary Brogan nee Whyte, Lisa Nolan, Mick Kearney, Paddy Mc Grath Dingle Road, Jim Murphy USA/Fassaugh Road, Patrick Spain Killala Road, Alan L'Estrange Killala Road, Eugene Naughton, Olive and Frank Carr, Terry Keegan and John Hannon. Thank you to all those who names may not be included in this list but whose contribution is gratefully appreciated.

Contents

Introduction

Many of the photographs in this book were originally stored away for many years in family albums, sideboards, old handbags, wardrobes, shoe boxes and attics. They were presented to the author for inclusion in this book by those people who have stood as guardians over them for many years. Every one of these photographs has its own story to tell. Each one is individual and unique. If a picture paints a thousand words then how many volumes can be filled with these alone? The people who presented these photographs are the children of those families who first moved into the new housing estate of Cabra West and the greater Cabra area from the late 1930's onwards. Their families mainly came from the city centre where living conditions were very often appalling.

Today many of these adult children are themselves parents, grandparents and even great grandparents. Through forced emigration in the 1950's, and 1960's quite a lot of them had no choice but to leave home and head off into the greater world of North America, South America, Australia, New Zealand, Germany, Britain, Switzerland and beyond. For those who stayed at home life offered little more than what their parents had endured. Throughout time some had lost touch with schoolfriends, old pals and neighbours for over fifty years. Through the use of the internet and the Cabra History.Com website they were able to reconnect with each other. As part of this reconnection they were able to share their memories, their stories and their family photographs with each other. Each photograph forms part of a greater picture of the lives of these people as they grew from childhood to adulthood. I am grateful to these people, many of whom I have never met, for entrusting me with their family photographs, stories and memorabilia of their childhood. Without their support and trust this book could not have been written.

Chapter One

Where did they come from?

In 1941 the Dublin City Manager reported to the Corporation Housing Committee that building work at present in the hands of Dublin Corporation covered the construction of approximately 1,400 dwellings, representing the completion of a programme of 2,155 houses undertaken the previous year. Arrangements were well under way at that time for the completion of the schemes at Crumlin North, Cabra West, Rialto and Donore Avenue, providing housing accommodation for an additional 2,256 families. Alderman T. Kelly, T.D. chairman of the Housing Committee said it was regrettable that the balance of the comprehensive housing programme adopted in 1938 might have to be deferred for a lengthy period due to the difficulties in obtaining the necessary building materials because of the war. The committee was also urged to proceed with the demolition of the slums in the Whitefriar Street area on the south side of the city. The above figures represent an estimated 4,500 families living in Dublin requiring new housing from their present dwellings. In order to qualify for a house from Dublin Corporation in 1941 a couple had to have a minimum of four children.

Trams in O'Connell Street.

On average the total number requiring new housing was therefore somewhere in the region of 24,000 people. The plan to re-house these families was a massive undertaking by a relatively new government struggling to rise up off its knees from the effects of the 1916 Insurrection, the Great War of 1914-1919, a War of Independence 1918-1921, a Civil War 1922-1923. In 1939 World War II was declared when Germany invaded Poland. In the midst of all this national and international turmoil the housing project for the families of Dublin city continued. Many of the people who first settled into Cabra West were poorly educated with some having received little or no education at all. They mainly came from very poor working class areas of Dublin City, areas that were severely neglected and overcrowded since early Victorian times. Large rats were frequently seen roaming through tenement houses and alleyways. Generations of families had lived in these conditions that had changed very little in the previous one hundred years. Families living in tenement houses shared one toilet between ten or more families. Many side streets were filled with overcrowded cottages where sanitation was almost unheard of.

Railway Street, Dublin

Few people had access to running water indoors and had to use candlelight or gaslight each night. During the war years the use of gas light was severely restricted to certain hours and one could be penalised for using it out of hours. In 1951 the Electricity Supply Board was still reminding people that electricity was being rationed. The recommended 'switching-on' time for using electricity for water heating was eight o'clock at night and 'switch-off' time was eight o'clock in the morning. People were being asked to help keep down the peak loads during the day when industrial and domestic demands were at their highest. These pictures show the demolition of the Railway Street area in Dublin city centre. Entire streets were being demolished and families forced to find alternative accommodation. Whole communities were being scattered and torn apart. Young children were dying from the effects of overcrowding in disease-ridden neighbourhoods. Other families were forced to make the move after their homes were destroyed in 1941 when German Luftwaffe pilots bombed the North Strand area of Dublin city. They were some of the first people to move into the newly-built houses on Swilly Road.

Railway Street, Dublin.

The new housing estates like Cabra that were springing up around the suburbs of Dublin offered new hope of a better way of life for many families. They moved out from the city with their families, friends and neighbours into an unknown future. With household goods and young children loaded onto handcarts rented from Granby Lane, with wheelbarrows and prams filled to capacity whole families headed off into a new life. There was a great feeling of excitement when the decision was finally made to move. With plenty of fresh air and open spaces for children to run and play they too were caught up in the excitement of the move. Everything was fresh and new. There were however a few families who were reluctant to make the move to the suburbs and even some who returned to the city way of life after a short stay in Cabra. It was usually the mother of the family who queued up at the Corporation Housing office in Jervis Street for the key to the new house. Families took to walking out to Cabra on Sunday afternoons to view the unfinished houses and to see where they were likely to live.

May and Sonny (centre) Doyle's tenement room in the Monto. Whole families lived in one room. Parents often shared their bed with the younger children. Nothing came easy or free to many families living in the squalor of Dublin tenement life.

A Monto family circa 1930 Bernard Coffey (with cap), Bridget Coffey, Paddy Fagan, Katie Fagan, Bridie Fagan and Paddy Foran.

A group of young newspaper boys from the inner city area of Dublin on a day trip to Rathfarnham Castle in 1918 courtesy of the Belvedere Newsboy's Club.

Chrissie McKeever, Chrissie Doyle, Gracie Doyle, Barney Doyle, Mousie Meehan and friends from the Monto circa 1936.

The Area 6 Warden Group who assisted in the rescue of victims from the wreckage of the North Strand bombings. Included in the photograph is Bernard Tonge, second on the right standing. He is the father of the Very Rev. Fr. Ivan Tonge P.P. Seville Place who served in the parish of Cabra West from 1972-1979.

The Five Lamps on the North Strand.

On the 30th May 1941 a tragic event took place that brought the reality of war straight into the homes of the people of Dublin. During the course of the war German bombers had off-loaded their deadly cargo of bombs over several areas of Ireland. In the previous year of 1940 bombs were dropped on County Wexford killing 3 persons. In that same year Carrickmacross in Monaghan, Dun Laoghaire and Sandycove in County Dublin were bombed. In 1941 more bombs were dropped on Drogheda, Duleek, Wexford, Carlow, Wicklow, the Curragh, Terenure, South Circular Road, the Phoenix Park, and the mainly working class area of Dublin City known as the North Strand. As a result of the damage caused to so many dwellings in this area of the city it was quickly decided to offer alternative housing to these families in the newly built areas of Kimmage and Cabra. As a result of the bombing on the North Strand area 28 people lost their lives, 90 people were treated for their injuries and at least 300 houses were damaged or destroyed. A public funeral was given for twelve of the bombing victims. The funeral service was held in St. Laurence O'Toole's Church in Seville Place. The church was packed to overflowing with relatives and friends of the deceased. A guard of honour, composed of members of St. Laurence O'Toole's Troop Catholic Boy Scouts, was drawn up around the coffins and afterwards walked with the remains to the cemetery where they were received by the Very Rev. Fr. T.B Ryan C.C. Cabra.

Bedsteads, armchairs and household furniture were purchased by those who could afford them and transported to their new homes in Cabra and elsewhere.

Any man with a horse and cart could make good money moving families and their possessions to the new housing estates that were springing up in the new suburbs of Dublin.

Like many other pawn offices in Dublin Rafter's Pawn Shop in Gardiner Street was a godsend to many families. The husband's suit or waistcoat could be pawned on Monday morning and redeemed on Friday. People pawned bedsheets, clothes, delph, prams, bicycles, wedding and engagement rings, musical instruments, shoes, ornaments and some even chanced wrapping a brick up in brown paper and pawning it.

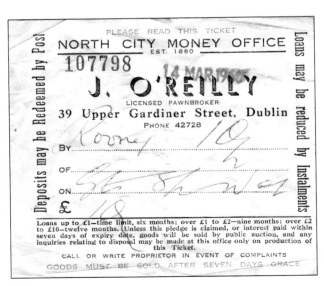

A Ticket from J O'Reilly's pawnshop in Gardiner Street.

Chapter Two

Into the West

In 1938 Dublin City Housing Department began working on the building of Cabra West. In 1941 the first section of houses to be complete was those in the area nearest to the Cabra Road. When new families began arriving in Cabra in the early 1940's they were greeted by one of the largest building sites in the new Free State. The majority of the houses were unfinished. When the rains fell it turned the whole area into one big mud bath that people had to walk through to get to their destinations. There were no walls or railings surrounding the houses at that particular time and no house had a bath installed. In some cases the new tenants were only allowed to have as few as two light bulbs in their house, one upstairs and one downstairs. There was only one electrical outlet or socket in the whole house and in most cases that was placed in the kitchen/living area of the house. Wild horses roamed freely around the estate.

Some houses had two bedrooms and a parlour while others had three bedrooms and a toilet downstairs. At a later stage a railings was placed in front of some houses and on others a wall with two pillars was put up for each house. The front and rear gardens were separated by wire fencing. In the early days each house had a bath placed in the front garden waiting for the plumbing team to arrive. Because of the war years there was a great shortage of materials of all sorts and so the baths were left in the garden for quite some time. The only means of public transport from the city centre was provided by the number twelve bus whose terminus was located on Quarry Road in Cabra East. This was a handy means of transport for those that lived within a close proximity of the bus route. Other families however were located up to half a mile away from the bus terminus and a journey into the city was almost a day's work in itself. The general feeling amongst the new tenants was one of delight at the prospect of a house of their own with running water, an indoor toilet and a bath.

This is a very early photograph of Broombridge taken from the upstairs bedroom window of number 325 Bannow Road in 1947. In the foreground is Mrs O'Kelly from 109 Killala Road.

A photograph of the Tolka River flowing through the archways of Cardiffbridge. In summer time children were brought here to paddle and swim. The bridge marked the boundary between Cabra West and Finglas.

Broombridge spanning the Royal Canal in Cabra West.

The Royal Canal and the Mullingar railway line joined at the hip. This canal pathway was the usual direction children took when heading off to the Ashtown Tin Box factory. They would steal the small metal lids that the factory produced and use them in various games.

Original hall door and windows.

Patrick Spain

'I can remember when we moved into our house in Cabra West. It was in the mid 1940's. We came from the North Strand. They were still building Broombridge Road and the upper part of Rathoath Road. The Nephin Road did not exist. To get to the Phoenix Park you had to go along Blindman's Lane by the side of the Deaf and Dumb Institute or St. Joseph's as it was then called. The Phoenix Park in those days had large stocks of coal and turf all over what is now the 15 acres. These were stocked up during the emergency as the Second World War was called in Ireland. The people like ourselves (the Spain's) that came from the North Strand were all bombed out during the war when a German plane unloaded its bombs on us. I remember when we were kids going for walks in the Park and we would always gather as much coal as we could and bring it home in shopping bags. In those days the gates of the park had guards that lived in the small lodges. They may have been called Rangers or something but they would check to see that we were not stealing the coal, which of course we were'.

A set of original windows with buntings

Most every house had a kitchen dresser but not every household had enough delph to fill it. This kitchen dresser dates from the early 1950's and belonged to Mrs Hayes who lived in number 21 Killala Road.

An enamelled breadbin was the traditional place where families kept their bread, when they had any that is. The most favoured bread was probably the Turnover and later on the Batch Loaf.

Many families washed everything from children to clothes in the kitchen sink. Carbolic soap and a scrubbing brush cleaned all. The meter for the gas was under the stairs in the coal-hole. Every trick in the book was used to do the gasman out of a few bob including the use of metal washers and home-made coins.

Chapter Three

Families

The O'Kelly family from Killala Road & and their cousins the Coote family in the 1950's. Families in Cabra as well as families in many other areas of Ireland very often consisted of three generations of parents, children and grandparents.

The Dunne Family 114 Cabra Road emigrated to Australia.

Eileen Meehan, Mary Bridget Mc Keever, Barney and Blacker Doyle with Willie and Jack Gorman were all born in the inner city. Most of them eventually moved to the suburbs.

The Jordan family 35 Mulroy Road 1947.

The little raggy boy on the left (Brendan Coffey) wears a pair of trousers made from a neighbour's coat. Very little went to waste as mother's strived to make do with what little they had. A secondhand pair of shoes or a dress may have come from a neighbour or handed down from a family member who had grown too big to wear them. In many families it was often a case of first up best dressed.

Anne, Mary, Catherine, Tony and June Coffey.

Ned & Kathleen Burke, 41 Broombridge Road with their children John, Anne and Vera. The Burkes moved to Cabra from the city in the early 1950's. Ned Burke was originally from County Tipperary and had served in the Irish Army.

Paddy & Chrissie Dunne from 114 Cabra Road with their daughter Claire who is the eldest of eight children. Their old house on the Cabra Road is still to this day named after Claire.

An old messenger bike.

Chapter Four

Neighbours

Neighbours from Lower Carnlough Road.

Many neighbours looked out for each other and helped where they could. They were almost like one big extended family. If there was sickness in a house or a mother was taken into hospital the neighbours very often shared the responsibility of looking after her children. Sometimes a dinner was put up for the husband when he came in from work. Of course some neighbours did have their differences, but when help was required, they were ready and available to step in to help out in times of need. In many cases it was simply a matter of asking for a loan of a cup of sugar or a shilling for the gas meter until the husband came home with his wages. Because many families came from similar backgrounds there seldom appeared to be any rivalry between neighbours. It was rarely a case of having to 'keep up' with the Jones because they were no better off.

The Dunnes, the Thompsons and the Brennan families from the Cabra Road gather together to wish a 'bon voyage' to Paddy Dunne as he prepares to leave Ireland in 1957. Tony Dunne from Australia is seen her with his little brother sitting on his lap. Here we see three families, the Dunne's from number 114 Cabra Road, the Brennan's from number 116 and the Thompson's from number 112 as they assemble together to wish a fond farewell to Paddy Dunne as he prepares to leave his home, neighbours, extended family and friends to travel with his wife and young children to Australia. Most families from the Cabra area have had similar experiences in their own homes as they stood back and watched some of their children, older siblings or neighbours putting on a brave face on their final night at home. Behind the smiling faces with their laughter and banter there was always the thought 'will they ever come back'? And of course there were all of the old fears of those leaving home wondering will things work out for them, what will eventually become of them and what if things don't work out for me? The neighbours never failed to give great support to those going and to those left behind.

Killala Road: Eileen Hayes, Mr Barry
and Mr Hayes with son Michael

Mr Hayes and Mr Coffey discussing football. Both men helped to
run the Soccer Road League. The two boys are Michael Hayes and
on the crossbar is Martin Coffey.

Mrs Coffey from Killala Road with two of her
fifteen children, June and Mary, on O'Connell Bridge.

Bried and Paddy McGrath from Dingle Road. They were both born in the same year, Paddy in January and Bried in December. The photograph was taken in the back garden of their house on Dingle Road about 1952. Mr and Mrs Mc Grath had nine children.

Brendan Coffey and John Burke.

May O'Gorman with Jimmy Hayes and young Barbara O' Gorman on her tricycle, Killala Road. Behind them is a van, probably belonging to Mr Crawley, a neighbour from number 19 Killala Road who had his own roof repair business.

Marie Whelan from lower Carnlough Road with her baby sister
Josie and two friends.

Rose & Mick Keegan from 131 Dingle Road.

Bernard and Mary Coffey from 36 Killala Road had 15 children.
Mr Coffey worked for most of his life as a Bank Porter with the
Hibernian Bank. He cycled to and from work everyday.

In many cases where a death occurred at home in Cabra a woman from the neighbourhood would come in to wash and lay out the deceased. She may even loan out clean white sheets to the family if none were available in the home. Sometimes this woman would bring one or two of her daughters with her to help out with the work. The corpse was usually laid out on the family bed surrounded by four lighted candles. A man was laid out wearing a brown habit and a woman, if she was a member of the 'Society of Children of Mary' could be laid out wearing a blue habit. The neighbours would gather around and offer whatever help they could in the way of tea and sandwiches of ham or cow's tongue. A wake was usually held in the home of the deceased and on the night before the funeral family, friends and neighbours would arrive at the house with more food and drink. While the death of a loved one was always considered a time of great sadness it was also a time for re-connecting with those who may have travelled from England or the country to attend the funeral. Many old acquaintances were renewed and all the latest gossip shared out. The saddest funeral was always that of a young child.

Going to Sunday Mass.

'There were lots of hobos then who'd come around. Me Ma' used to always put them on the end of the stairs and give them a cup of tea. I think they were war veterans, you know what I mean. They were fellas that were affected in the war and they couldn't get accommodation or anything like that. They had nowhere to go. A lot of ex army men would come home from the war. The family didn't want them and they may have been shell-shocked or something like that. Hairy Lemon and that, they were all ex army men I think. I think that's why me Ma' kind of looked after them. I remember one ould fella used to always sit on the end of the stairs with a cup of tea and bread and butter. Me mother always took somebody in, she loved waifs and strays. I think in them days most people did, they looked after each other. They shared what they had. You could leave your door open. That's if you had a door and it wasn't on the fire. One day we caught a mouse on Rathoath Road and we had him in a bottle. There was a herd of cows coming up Rathoath Road and just to see what would happen we threw the mouse in among the cows. They just rambled over it but they didn't kill it, the thing actually lived. I think we drowned it in the horse trough then after that'.

Olive Jackson, Kay Lynch, Mrs Lynch, Noel Lynch, unknown,
and May Clarke at the wedding of Kay's cousin on Mulroy Road
1953.

Patty Carey from 46 Killala Road.

Mrs and Mr O'Kelly of 109 Killala Road.

Large families of up to fifteen children were not unusual in Cabra. Some families went on to have over twenty children. Many of these large families were crowded into a house with two bedrooms. Others more fortunate were given a house with three bedrooms. Some parents used the downstairs parlour as a third bedroom. The parlour was usually kept for entertaining visitors. Children were forbidden to use the parlour as it sometimes housed the good delph, the family china, ornaments and perhaps the only good chair in the house.

Breda Burke (centre) 41 Broombridge Road
playing with her two pals in the garden.

James Kavanagh of 581 Carnlough Road.

Rose O'Driscoll.

Rose O'Driscoll is fondly remembered by many people in Cabra West for the beautiful and simplistic poetry that she wrote. She wrote verses for Christmas cards and performed poetry readings in the Parish Centre. A piece of her work was actually aired on the Gay Byrne radio show. By all accounts Rose was a good and kind friend to all. Rose moved into Cabra West in 1943 with her young family. She originally came from a rural background with her roots firmly planted in County Kildare. However, Rose took Cabra West and its people into her heart and settled in well with her new neighbours and friends. She lived with her husband and six children on Carnlough Road. A great legacy that Rose left behind to the people of Cabra West was that of her poetry.

Lisa Byrne 42 Killala Road.

Mr O'Kelly 109 Killala Road at the Cabra Baths 1954. In the background a young boy can be seen in his swimming trunks. Due to the lack of swimmers in the pool it is possible that this photograph was taken on a Sunday morning.

Mrs O'Kelly at the Cabra swimming baths in 1954. She is standing at the shallow end where the younger boys had to swim and paddle. The fields in the background most probably belonged to the Craigie family. Young boys would go nesting in the trees in search of birds eggs. The eggs were never taken out of the nest. The boys would be content to see who could count the most eggs.

Chapter 5

More Neighbours

Mick and Etna Kearney from Carnlough Road.

Paddy & Maggie Dunne from Dingle Road.

Bernard Coffey, 36 Killala Road joined the British army in 1930. He served on the island of Malta for many years. He was later transferred to Palestine and then to Cairo in Egypt where he became involved in the Arab uprising of 1936. He was a member of the 22nd Cheshire Regiment and was stationed originally in Chester, England. As a young boy Bernard sold newspapers barefooted around the streets of Dublin and was a member of the Belvedere Newsboys Club.

Fran and Danny Mitchell.

Jim Murphy from Fassaugh Road at his army graduation ceremony in the Curragh. Jim is seated in the front row third from the right.

Molly O'Brien of 34 Killala Road on her 90th birthday.

'I started school when I was five years old. I started in Gardiner Street School, beside Gardiner Street chapel. The Sisters of Charity ran that school. You had to go down a laneway to it. We had lay teachers and nuns. For two years I was going to the Eye and Ear Hospital and at that time we didn't have the Blue Card (Medical Card). I had to wear glasses and we were living on the North Circular Road at the time. I worked in North Williams Street School. I was eighteen years there. I was also eighteen years working on Iona Road cleaning houses and I was only thirteen years old at the time I started. Then I went to work in William Street School. I had seven classrooms, a corridor, two cloakrooms and a big long passage to clean. That all had to be done on Friday night and Saturday. You were paid of a Saturday. Sadie Kilcullen of Killala Road worked with me. I then went to work in Grangegorman Hospital. On our first winter in Cabra there was a snow blizzard and you had to get shovels to get up to Mass on Sunday. Some of the men would go up to the Phoenix Park and cut down trees for firewood. In some other places you could get a bit of coal. We had to break up the dresser. We had a chest of drawers and that had to be broken up for the fire, to dry your clothes.'

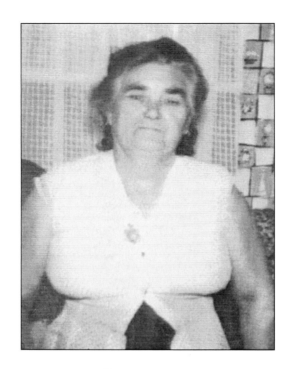

Elizabeth Moore.

The Bryan family from Inver Road.

Vera Coffey SRN

Many young girls from the Cabra area left home and took up a career in nursing in hospitals all over England. Girls who were successful in getting jobs in England often sent word back to their pals at home. During the 1950's and 1960's good paying jobs in Ireland were few and far between. Thousands of young people emigrated to England in search of a dream. Some of the girls would live in hostels run by the Catholic Church. The lads would sometimes end up sharing a bed in some lodging house where drinking, smoking and girls were forbidden. Vera Coffey worked in Williams and Woods Ltd sweet factory before heading off to England.

Anne and Bernard Coffey.

'I remember we didn't have a bath because it was in the summer that they came along. The workmen came along and put all the baths into the front garden turned upside down waiting for the plumbers. I must have been about four and a half or five years old when I went to school. One day when I came home from school the bath was in the front garden and turned upside down. I remember standing on it and it being hot because it was so warm that summer. A few of us were scutting behind a bread van and it went up around Rathoath Road and we dropped off at the corner where the old horse trough used to be. We then got up on the wall of Saint Joseph's School to walk along it and the wall collapsed. There was a great big bee's nest inside the wall. Now I had read Beano and Dandy comics and you'd see the bees chasing the kids and they would always jump into a pool of water so the bees can't get them. The swarm of bees chased me and the two Quinns down onto Killala Road. A gang of lads were playing cards in the middle of the field. I saw the lads and I ran in amongst them. You should have seen them scatter'.

Jim Murphy from Fassaugh Road 1953.

Above is a photograph of Jim Murphy and the old C.I.E. office in O'Connell Street, taken in 1953. In later years this little office was used as a tourist information office. Previous to that it was the main point for all timetables for the old Dublin trams and buses. The two busmen are probably a duo of conductor and driver waiting to pick up their bus. The last bus from town pulled out from its terminus at half past eleven when the bus inspector blew on his whistle. The number 22 and 22A bus left from the Carlton Cinema in O'Connell Street. The number 39 and 38 bus left from Aston Quay. The first set of buses headed up Parnell Square and the North Circular Road. The second two buses headed down the quays and made their way up along to Blackhall Place and Manor Street. This route eventually took them up to Rathoath Cross and Cabra. To the right of the photograph is Burton's Tailor shop situated on the corner of O'Connell Street and North Earl Street. To the left can be seen the doorway to the famous and now demolished Nelson's Pillar. Above the doorway is a sign showing the opening hours and cost of entry, six old pennies. Each weekend Jim Murphy cycled a sixty mile round trip on his bicycle from Cabra to the Curragh army camp.

Jack Lynch, 90 Drumcliffe Road with his C.I.E. horse in 1961.

Tommy 'Tucker' and Mamie Jordan from Annamoe Drive 1963.

Phibsboro Postal Delivery at Christmas

'My father is Tommy (Tucker) Jordan and he was the postman for the Cabra Road for most of his life. At Christmas time the Da' and most of the regular postmen were kept in the office to sort out the mail. It was usually the temporary postmen (mostly students) who went out on the deliveries. The regulars like my Dad hated this because they wanted to get out on their walks to get their Christmas boxes. The hours were very long in the sorting office. The men had to sort from five o'clock in the morning until about nine o'clock at night. My Dad and his pals would slip over the road to Doyle's pub for a few pints when they got the chance. One time I had to fetch the old man from the sorting office because he was too drunk to get home on his own. Now when he did manage to get out on his walk between the 22nd and 24th of December I would go with him to help him deliver the Christmas cards and letters.

Postman Tucker Jordan and his son Richard 1963.

When people would see me with him they would also give me a few bob. One time he realised that his tips were getting less so he sent me home. One year I came home from England for the Christmas and when I went down the Cabra Road looking for him I found him half jarred sitting on the basement steps of a house singing his head off. He blamed the people for bringing him in for a tot. Well I eventually got him home and there was still quite a bit of mail in his bag. I put on his tunic and went out to finish the job for him. When I got back he had the cheek to ask me how much tips I had collected. I never told him. The shops on the Cabra Road used to give him the Christmas dinner and Downey's pub supplied the beer. One year the dentist on the Cabra Road took out all his teeth and gave him a new set of false ones for a Christmas present'.

Jim Murphy and Nelson's demise 1966.

At 2am on the 8th March 1966 a very large explosion awakened the people of Dublin. At first it was thought by some to be a possible escape from Mountjoy Prison on the nearby North Circular Road. To others it seemed as if a ship carrying explosives had blown up along the quayside. It was in fact the demise of Admiral Nelson's Pillar situated in the centre of Dublin's famous O'Connell Street. A group of former IRA men later claimed responsibility. In 1966 the Irish Republic celebrated the 50th anniversary of the 1916 Easter Rising. The Pillar was the main meeting point for both Dublin and country people. Under the large clock belonging to Clery's department store in O'Connell (on the right of the photograph) was another great meeting place for people. Many a romance began and finished under this clock.

Patty Lynch with her first cousin Peggy Shields from Drimnagh, Mrs Lily Lynch & her sister Nellie Shields Drimnagh.

'The birth of the Bogies...when I started school in the convent the land that is now the Bogies was a wood, that land was owned by the nuns. It was sold to the Corporation, they set about clearing the land, the trees were cut down and cut into logs and they were then loaded on to the carriages called bogies. This became our playground when school ended for the day. I remember saying to Jerry Clarke, are you going to play on the bogies after school, we used to play cowboys. It became known as the Bogies after the wood was cut down and the carriage removed. I always lay claim that the kids of the forties gave the name to that park through playing on the narrow gauge rail line'.

Mike Judge from Bannow Road and Billy Coote.

Billy Coote was originally from 24 Phoenix Street in Stoneybatter. He left school shortly after his eleventh birthday. He went to sea as a cabin boy when he was thirteen. Having sailed around the world Billy eventually enlisted in the British Army. He was posted to Charles Fort near Kinsale in County Cork where he took up boxing. He weighed in as a welterweight and was seldom beaten. In 1919 Billy Coote was enlisted into the Connaught Rangers Infantry Division and shipped out to Jullunder in India. During his time there in 1920 word reached the regiment of the atrocities being committed in Ireland by the Black and Tans. Some of the Irishmen decided to protest at this by refusing to carry out their regimental duties until something was done about the situation back home.

Billy Coote (extreme right) with his family in Cabra.

The mutineers were rounded up and confined to an encampment where one of their number died from fever due to the terrible condition of the place. Private James Daly was considered by the authorities to be the main ringleader. He was court-martialled and executed by firing squad for his part in the mutiny. Billy Coote was one of the soldiers who went on a committee in protest and he too was later court-martialled. He was sentenced to a number of years in prison and was shipped off to Maidstone Prison in England where he served 11 months and 18 days. In 1922 the Connaught Rangers were disbanded and sent home at the request of General Michael Collins. Part of the deal involved the mutineers forfeiting their entitlement to a British pension. The Irish government stepped in and gave them a pension. Billy Coote worked as a boiler man in the Botanic Gardens for many years and later progressed to become a gardener. In 1942 Billy and his family moved to 57 Inver Road in Cabra West. In 1970 Billy witnessed the return to Ireland of the remains of Private James Daly who was eventually laid to rest in Tyrrellspass in County Westmeath. Billy Coote died just short of his 83rd birthday in 1973. The British Army however never returned the boxing medals and trophies belonging to Billy to his family.

Anthony Mitchell

Anthony Mitchell lived in 227 Rathoath Road in Cabra West. He was a cattle drover all of his working life with Ganley's in Prussia Street. His brother John Mitchell was also a cattle drover. Anthony's father was the caretaker in the cattle market in Prussia Street and lived in a small house belonging to the market.

Mrs Lynch 90 Drumcliffe Road, Cabra West.

Two cattle drovers.

Paddy (Danny) Mitchell and his sister Peg from number
one Killala Road walking along O'Connell Street in 1955.

Chapter Six

Children

The bigger the family the bigger the pram. Prams such as the one pictured above served a multi purpose role in many households. They were used for transporting everything from several babies to groceries and sometimes the transportation of bags of turf or coal.

Catherine Coffey 1959.

Martin Branagan from Lower Carnlough Road.

'Me Ma used to keep the cinders and she'd wash them. Then stack up the fire in the evening time so that there'd be a nice glowing red fire for when me Da would come in from work and that. Everything used to get put on it. There were ould shoes used to go on it; they were a great man for it, shoes and bits of lino. Anything that burned, even potato skins and cabbage leaves went on it mixed with the cinders. That used to hold it all together and you just got a red glow. It saved the coal. It was great for toasting bread on. We used to go down to the cattle market on Wednesdays. You had the cattle market and the pig market as well. You'd get an odd penny for helping the cattle men or drovers. All the cows were hooshed along the roads then. Other times me Da would send us down with a boxcar to get the cow dung for his garden. He used to put that in his vegetable garden'.

This is John and Anne Burke from 41 Broombridge Road. On the ground is a little plastic water pistol. The little girl is holding a 'Piggy' in her left hand. This was used in the game of 'Piggy Beds'. Usually it was the girls that played this game. On the odd occasion boys would sometimes join in. Skipping with a rope was also a very popular game.

June, Jo, Patty, Kevin, Kieran and Dessie O'Neill
from 140 lower Carnlough Road.

Happy children very often reflected a happy home where the children felt safe and loved. Feeding a large family was a mammoth task for parents, many of whom would have gone without food in order to feed their children. Christmas time would have been especially hard on these families. Parents would take out loans from moneylenders, the Jew man or from some credit company to ensure that each child was catered for on Christmas morning. The Providence cheque was very popular with most people because it could be cashed in most clothing shops.

The O'Kelly's from Killala Road.

The O'Neill's from 140 lower Carnlough Road.

Joan Mc Grath front left with her brother Paddy and pals.

Michael Hayes with Noel and Billy Coffey.

Deirdre and Maureen Price lived with their family in the
'Keyhole' on lower Carnlough Road

Frank Stynes of 37 Mulroy Road 1967.

Liam and Eamonn O'Kelly with their cousin June sitting on the lock gate at Reilly's Bridge on the Royal Canal near Cabra West. The photograph was taken by Mr O'Kelly in 1948. Many children from Cabra claimed the canal as their own to swim and fish in. It was along the canal bank that families strolled on a Sunday afternoon where they could pick blackberries and collect mushrooms.

These boys from Dingle Road are Eamonn Doyle, Willie Hughes,
Joseph Casserly, Q Keegan (?) and Sean Cunningham.

The Burke family of 41 Broombridge Road.

Willie Kavanagh and Martin Coffey from Killala Road 1956.

Louie and Willie Lynch from Drumcliffe Road
with their dog Rover.

Noel Coffey.

The Raggy Boy

James Rogers

'I'm on a spiritual journey looking for a raggy boy.
I want to hold him in my arms and say my last goodbye.
I want to look into his eyes and wipe away a tear.
And to tell him on his journey through life,
There's nothing he should fear.
So here I am back on Killala Road, looking for that raggy boy.
Will I see him running with his hoop?
Or playing with a broken toy?
Just then, a voice said 'mister don't you know it's rude to stare'.
I turned around to reply but there was no one there.
And as a Celtic mist engulfed me, a vision set me free.
The raggy boy I was looking for was the raggy boy in me'.

Learning to go on his first bike.

'As you know Christmas time in Cabra brought out the religious boys selling all sorts of things. Well in our hallway we had a statue of Blessed Martin. A knock came to the door one day and there was this fellow selling religious stuff. So when this fellow tried to sell these items to my father the Da' told him we were not a religious family. The man asked the Da' if he wasn't religious why did he have a statue of Blessed Martin in the hall. My Father said "do you know, the man who sold me that told me it was Sugar Ray Robinson the boxer'. The man went away shaking his head and I was on the floor with the laughter'.

Danny Mitchell from
Killala Road on his new tricycle.

Tony O'Reilly on the right from 75 Fassaugh Avenue.

Chapter Seven

Best Pals

1961 Brendan Jordan and Tony Sheridan from Annamoe Drive. Every young boy or girl from Cabra had a best pal. Sometimes these friendships only lasted a couple of hours but in many cases they lasted a lifetime. Tony Sheridan later died in an accident near where this photograph was taken.

Annie Bolger, Anna Donovan & Eileen Hayes.

Betty O'Neill from Cabra West in Wexford 1954.

These two football buddies dressed in their Sunday best are Michael Whelan and Tommy Swann. They are holding onto their football boots and shin guards. This photograph was taken in 1952.

Ella Bryan with David and Gerard Mc Elligott on Inver Road.

Ella & Bernard Bryan with Breda Mc Elligott
and Mary Mc Keever on Inver Road.

Bridget Hayes with Paula Price and Florrie Shortt.

The best of Cabra pals.
All of the girls are wearing great big ribbons in their hair.

Marie Whelan & Mary Clarke with friends.

A group of Boy Scouts from Cabra West on camp in Skerries about 1953. The 53rd Scout Troop C.B.S.I was based in Finbarr's Hall and they performed the Guard of Honour for the opening of the new church. Mr 'Fiddler' Kelly from Carnlough Road was the troop leader. Canon Burke would often visit the campsite in the grounds of Ardgillan Lodge near Skerries. One night Mr Kelly went for a pint and when he returned the boys had stitched up the front of his tent for a laugh. Amos Walsh was the previous leader.

Fr Kavanagh with Mary Clarke, Betty O'Neill, Rosanna Crowe, Carmel Cummins, Maureen Quinn, Olive Jordan and Kay Lynch 1952-53.

Eugene Rooney with Shay and Noel Jordan Annamoe 1974.

'My name is Shay Jordan and I lived on Annamoe Drive. My best pal is Eugene Rooney. We left home together in the 1950's and took the boat to England to find work. We ended up in a lodging house in Birmingham where we shared the same room. It was so cold that we went to bed in our overcoats. We were not allowed to cook in the room but we had a gas ring and a small kettle. One time we bought a tin of Irish stew and I put a few sausages in with it and boiled the lot in the kettle. We nearly got thrown out one time because the toilet was out of bounds. All we had was the wash-up jug and basin just like in the cowboy films. We had no choice but to pee in one of these. Rooney then threw the lot out of the window into the yard. Unfortunately the old landlady came out the back door and nearly clobbered the lot. If you have ever seen the film 'The Lavender Hill Mob' well she was the image of that landlady. The Irish got a rough deal over there in those days. The signs on the doors said "No Irish-No Coloureds - No Dogs".

Mr Kehoe from Bannow Road with May Clarke, Kay Lynch and friends in the Bogie Fields. Mr Kehoe was a great man for the G.A.A.

Thomas Crawley, Michael Hayes and their pal fishing for pinkeens in the Silverspoon. This was a section of the Tolka River behind the Cabra open-air baths. It was also a great spot for catching frogs and grasshoppers.

Rosanna Crowe and Betty O'Neill 1953.

Betty O'Neill, Olive Jordan and
Rosanna Crowe from Cabra West
in Wexford 1953

Margaret Brannigan and Noel Lynch

Noel Lynch and friend 1953.

Jimmy Rogers and Tom Mc Kenna.

Ancient Order of Hibernia dance hall 17th November 1952.

Best pals.

'Every Sunday night I'd go down to O'Connell Street and I'd buy black market cinema tickets because you couldn't get in anywhere. So there'd be people standing outside the G.P.O. selling tickets for the Adelphi or somewhere and you'd pay over the odds for the tickets. They were people who had bought the tickets earlier and were reselling them at black market prices. One of the first times I went to the pictures with a girl was to the Adelphi Cinema and when we went to go in the head usher wouldn't let her in because you had to be over eighteen to get in then'.

Dingle Road early 1960's.

L-R: Thomas Ryan, Dennis Doyle, Christy McKeever, Noel Doyle, Patsy Dempsey, Brian Brady and Eamonn Doyle.

'I didn't get to see the Beatles because I couldn't get tickets. I saw the Rolling Stones alright. I think it was on the Carlton or the Adelphi. 'Lugs' Brannigan was there. Jagger was down on the stage, right on the edge of the stage teasing the girls. You know the way rock singers do. Lugs was there telling him to go back. I used to love going to those concerts. So I saw the Bachelors, Dickie Rock and Cliff Richard with the Shadows in the Boxing Stadium on the South Circular Road. They were in the ring. Dickie Rock was on. He was a big star even by Irish standards then. The Bachelors were a big group too, three guys with their harmonicas. Cliff Richard and the Shadows were the main group'.

Chapter 8

Communions and Confirmations

Coyle's hat shop where boys bought their school caps.

First Holy Communion and Confirmation days were always a time of great excitement for children. Again this was a time of great financial stress on parents as they had to beg, steal and borrow money for the children's outfits. Young boys and girls from Cabra West usually made their First Communion in the little chapel belonging to Saint Catherine's convent school. The girls were dressed in a white dress and veil. Some girls also wore white gloves. The boys wore a collar and tie with a short trouser two-piece suit and school cap. They had a rosette and medal pinned onto the left hand side of their coat. Each child had a small white prayer book. Faces were scrubbed and hairs washed with great ceremony for the child's big day. Coyle's Outfitters in Aungier Street was the usual place to go for your school cap.

Anne Coffey on her First Holy Communion Day.

Liam O'Kelly from 109 Killala Road
making his First Holy Communion 1948.

Souvenir of First Communion

received _____ First Communion on _____ 19 53

Baptised _____ Confirmed _____

_____ Priest

Each young boy was given a First Holy Communion certificate to remember his 'special' day. On the back of this certificate they had to write their Holy Communion promise; 'I promise to say my prayers every night'. The girls also were given a similar certificate.

SOUVENIR OF FIRST COMMUNION

Received First Holy Communion on _____ 19___

at Dominican Convent, Cabra, Dublin

Girl's souvenir of First Holy Communion.

It was usual when young children made their First Holy Communion or Confirmation to have their father or maybe both parents take them around to visit their relations. Before heading off however the children would do a round of the neighbours' houses first. It was always customary for the neighbours and families to give the children some money. This custom may have originated from a long time ago when families and neighbours would help out a family in need and especially at Communion or Confirmation time. By the end of the day the little communicant would be footsore and weary. The father in many cases would have been given a glass or two of whiskey or stout on his arrival at the home of his relatives. So by the end of the day he too was the worse for wear. Most every young boy and girl was taken into a photographic studio in town to have their special day remembered with a nice photograph. Almost every street in Dublin city centre had a photographic studio.

Paddy Mc Grath 114 Dingle Road, Cabra West.

'My Name is Paddy Mc Grath and I made my Confirmation in 1950. I had to go to the photographic studio in Henry Street to have my picture taken. I was born in December of 1939. We lived in 114 Dingle Road in Cabra West during the late 1940's and 1950's. There were nine children altogether in our house. Bried was the eldest, then Paddy (that's me), Marie, Chrissie, Michael, Joan, Noel, John and Francis. I went to Saint Finbarr's School and Mister Murphy was the headmaster. His cane on a cold morning would soon wake you up. I also remember 'Hitler' Mc Guire with his ruler. He left welts on your hands and put the fear of God into everyone. I remember Mister O'Halloran with his leather strap and his tongue hanging out but he never really hurt us at all. 'Lanky' Williams was another teacher we had. He slept all day and never paid attention to anyone. When I was at school Alfie Byrne was the Lord Mayor of Dublin. He introduced the current buns into the schools and we got them on Wednesday. On seeing the Church of the Precious Blood it always reminds me of how I used to end up outside the Church every time because I used to faint inside.

First Holy Communion Medal.

I used to go to the Navan Road to get the rhubarb every week for the Ma'. Looking back now it was all good fun. Cabra had the best football team in Dublin. The name of it was Saint Bernard's. In the 1955-56 season under 16's we won the treble, the league, the cup and the juvenile cup. Our main rivals were Home Farm, Johnville and Carrow Celtic. We used to love playing at Home Farm's ground because they had showers (lovely). Two seasons earlier we won the under 14's title beating none other than The Leprechauns. They were managed by Dickie Giles whose son John was starting out on the road to fame. He played inside left. Our manager was Paddy O'Brien from Carnlough Road, bike and all. Our team was as follows: Bartle O'Brien, Donal Ryan (Capt), Sonny Carroll, Freddie Sweeney, Paddy Mc Grath (me), Noel O'Loughlin, Pat Ratcliffe, Mick White, Jimmy Morrissey, Nedser English and Gino O' Reilly. I remember Mister Groves from Killala Road used to sell the newspapers outside Eason's in O'Connell Street. At Christmas time we all looked forward to going to the parties at the Grove's house where we could stuff ourselves with loads of food.

We had Father Burke as our Parish Priest in the Precious Blood; one hour Mass. Father 'Flash' Kavanagh only took ten minutes. That was the Mass all the young ones went to. We had an open air swimming pool where we used to go every summer. It was just past Broombridge and across the fields and it was free. My grandfather used to run the Cattle Market in Prussia Street. He was Eddie Mitchell from Rathoath Road. On our way down to the Manor Picture House we used to go into his house to get the price of the pictures, if we were lucky. Cabra was a great place to grow up, no money but good friends. To name but a few of many: Mick Mitchell, Alfie and Brendan Groves (Killala Road), Willie Hill, Oscar French, Paddy Cahill and the Lennons from Dingle Road.

One thing I remember well in the late 50s is when television came to Cabra West. Before the inauguration of RTE we had a telly on Dingle Road but the screen was full of snow so we couldn't see anything only shadows. The engineers used to come to the house and raise the aerial up to the sky and you had to tell them when the picture was clear. Down they came, took your money and off they went. The picture would be alright for about half an hour and then the snow would come back again. The whole place was full of aerials high up in the air and no pictures. Two doors up from us lived another McGrath family and the boy's names were the same as ours Paddy, Michael and Noel.

Confirmation Medal.

Well, Michael was a great footballer who played for Home Farm with Liam Whelan and he was then playing for Blackburn Rovers. The teams in the 1960 Cup Final in Wembley were Blackburn Rovers -v- Wolves and Michael McGrath was playing. In our house everyone was trying to watch the match through the snow. Wolves won 3-0 and their first goal was an own goal scored by none other than Mick McGrath. Needless to say his mother wasn't too happy about that, nor for that matter were the rest of us on Dingle Road'.

Mary Brogan.

Charlie Brogan from 104 Killala Road.

'My name is Charlie Brogan and I was born on the 22 January in 1951. I was actually born in our front parlour. We lived in 104 Killala Road and I am the only one in the family who was actually born at home. My siblings are as follows; Sean born in 1935 and now lives in Australia, My sister Nellie was born in 1937 and is now deceased, My brother Thomas was born in 1938 and he too is deceased, my sister Claire was born in 1940 and now lives in England, my sister Esther was born in 1942 and also lives in England, my brother Michael was born in 1945 and lives in Kildare. Michael was best pals with Gerry O'Shea from Killala Road who was also known as 'Glenn Lee' of Beaumont Hospital Radio fame. I remember the walks up to Broombridge or Broomer as we used to call it. We would always get a feed of blackberries on the way along the canal. My aunt Eileen is one of the Royalettes (extreme right) in Bridie Hentschel's wedding photo. My mother helped to deliver Mrs O'Shea's twins. They were great years and we'd swing on the lampposts and play kick-the-can until it would be nearly dark. We also lived near the L'Etranges and my eldest brother Sean was pals with Dykie L'Estrange'.

Frances Mc Grath with Fr O'Farrell.

Tony Coffey (left) with his Dad and cousin Brian Burke.

Tony Dunne from the Cabra Road makes his Confirmation from Saint Peter's School. A boy's Confirmation outfit usually consisted of a shirt and tie, a short trouser suit, a school cap, gloves, knee length socks, a three quarter length overcoat and a pair of new shoes

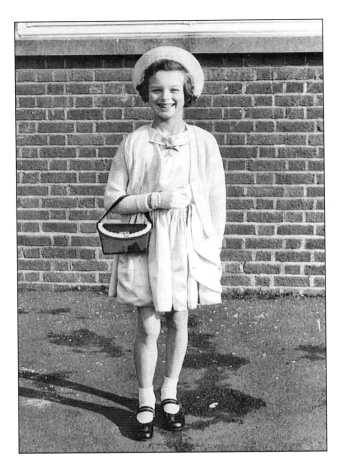

Anne Coffey's Confirmation Day.

'We actually made our Confirmation in our school. The girls and boys had to walk with each other. It was the same for the Communion. For our Confirmation we had to wear our school uniform. I think that was the first year that it was brought in that you had to wear your uniform. Then we had to go home and change into the good clothes that we wore going around the relations and neighbours. I had a pink satin dress that my sister made for me and I later wore that at her wedding. When you walked up the church a girl and boy had to walk with each other. I remember going around the houses on Killala Road and Mrs Quinlan gave me a shilling. My father brought me to see his relations'.

Liam O'Kelly from 109 Killala Road
in his Confirmation outfit in 1952.

First Holy Communion girl Anne Burke
from 41 Broombridge Road.

Vera Burke.

Eileen Hickey.

First Holy Communion girls from Killala Road.

Confirmation boys from Dingle Road in 1949 are Brian Brady, Dickie Rock, Willie Hughes and Eamon Doyle.

Noel Coffey in his Confirmation suit.

Danny Mitchell, Christie Quinn and Thomas Crawley from Killala
Road making their First Holy Communion.

Marie & Ella Bryan from Inver Road.

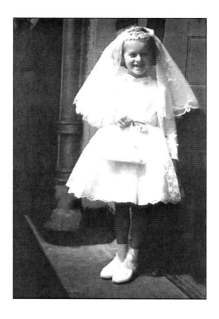

Anne Coffey visiting her relations.

Chrissie Mc Grath in her Confirmation outfit.

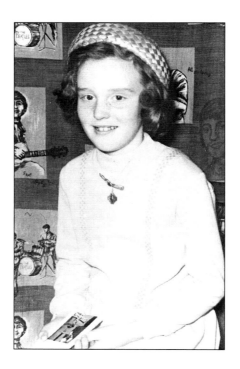

Vera Burke.

First Holy Communion group with Father Green.

Vera Coffey.

'Mrs O'Brien from next door made my First Holy Communion dress and it was made from coffin lining. Her daughter worked for a place that made habits for the dead and also stitched up the lining for coffins. I didn't know at the time what it was made from and my bag was the same. It was one of those little drawstring bags. My aunt bought me my coat and it was pink and for years that was my favourite colour. I still have my Communion Medal. My mother gave it to me a few years back. We were up in the Convent Chapel and we went into the Convent dining room for breakfast. I don't know what else we had for breakfast but I know we had ice cream because we never got ice cream at home'.

Chapter 9

Schools in the Cabra Area

Saint Catherine's convent school on Rathoath Road in Cabra West was run by the Dominican Order of nuns. They first settled in the area in 1812.

'I started school in the Convent School in about 1953. I had Sister Mary Consalvo first and then I had a Miss O'Connor. There was a Miss O'Malley and then there was Miss Byrne. I think Miss O'Connor lived facing the church in Phibsborough. I remember going in to get my Communion clothes and she was on the bus. I seen her getting off the bus and going into a house so I assumed she lived down there. On my first day I remember running out of my classroom. I remember my Ma bringing me up to the school and the nun bringing us into the class. The parents came into the class and all. When me Ma went out the door I ran out after her, screaming and shouting. The nun grabbed me by the arm and put me sitting in the seat saying everything would be alright. I think that's what turned me against school'.

The Dominican Convent Grotto.

Dominican Convent Girls 1976.

Anne Coffey School Photo.

Nuns and girls from the Dominican Convent School.

REPORT
of the Conduct and Progress in Studies of

Mrs. _Ingrid Hentschel_   Class. _Form III_ _Anna_   Term, 19. _20_

SUBJECT			Application in Class Work	Place 100	SUBJECT	Application in Class Work	Marks 100
1. Religious Knowledge			Ex.	100 A	8. Speech Training	V. G.	
2. Irish	Oral		Ex.	100 A	9. Physical Education	V. G.	
	Written				10. Singing	V. G.	
	Spelling		Ex.	90 A	11. Art	V. G.	
3. English	Written		V. G.	A	12. Crafts	V. G.	
	Reading		Ex.	100 A	13. Piano		
	Poetry		Ex.	100 A	_Nature Study_	V. G.	A
	Writing		Ex.	98 A	1. Conduct	V. G.	
	Spelling		Ex.	838	2. Tidiness	V. G.	
4. Arithmetic			Ex.	818	3. Manners	V. G.	
5. Tables					4. Punctuality	V. G.	
6. History					5. Attendance		
7. Geography							

Parents will kindly take special notice of this Report, and thus co-operate with the Religious in the education of their Children.

REMARKS _Ingrid is most satisfactory_   Sister M. Leontia O.P.   Principal

School Re-opens on _September 2nd_

Parents are earnestly requested to secure **punctual** return of their children on **date** of re-opening

School Report.

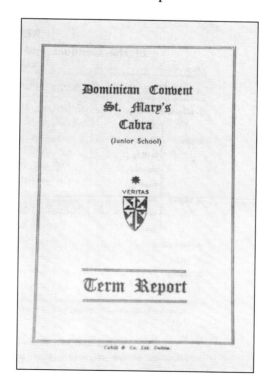

School term report.

AM I READY FOR SCHOOL?

Is my face clean?
Is my neck clean?
Are my ears clean?
Are my knees clean?
Have I brushed my hair
Have I cleaned my teeth?
Have I washed my hands?
Am I neat and tidy?
Have I cleaned my shoes?
Have I a clean handkerchief?

If the answer to all these questions is
Yes," then I am ready for school.

5

Am I Ready for School?

THE TOYSHOP

Once there was a little girl who started
out with her mother on a sunny summer day
to visit the town. She was just as happy as
she could be, for they were going to the
Toyman's shop, and she had a silver piece
of money in her pocket to buy a toy there.

"Here I go with a hop, hop, hop,
All the way to the Toyman's shop,

she sang over and over as she danced
beside her mother.

On the way they met a little boy who
ing with his mother to visit the town

26

The Toyshop.

118

Sister Mary Martin

The young children attending the Convent School were always encouraged by the Nuns to bring a penny or silver paper to school each Friday for to the black babies in Africa.

'We had to bring in money for the Black Babies. On the door they had a chart like a ladder and they would pin a little paper black baby onto it. As we all gave our pennies the baby would go up another step on the ladder. Our mothers didn't have money for themselves let alone give you money for the black babies'.

'Many's the time we had to go down to the soup kitchen to get a feed. The lady who ran the place (beside the nun's) was named Theresa. When I started work at the local shops she used to come in at the end of each day and we would give her the scraps to make a stew'.

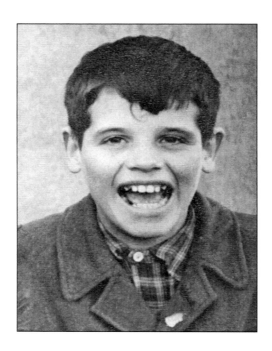

Noel Coffey

'We used to go down to the Mater Hospital after school. I was in Saint Finbarr's School at the time and we used to go down to the Mater to visit the dead. Meself and me pals, about four or five of us would go. There was 'Jaycee' Quinn, Christie Quinn, Danny Mitchell, 'Fat' Crawley and 'Sabbo' Norton. That was our gang. We'd walk down to the dead house after school because there was always someone laid out. We couldn't always see into the coffins because some of them were up on a high stand. We used to give each other a bunk up and we were after the pennies. What they used to do when you went there if the eyes were slit open they'd put pennies on them so people wouldn't see the eyes open. Sometimes we couldn't reach up into the coffin. We'd put our hands up because we couldn't see and we'd be feeling. 'Ah that's the toe...go to the other end'. We used to go down and there used to be Nuns praying and they'd be praying at the coffin. We'd be saying 'when are they going to finish praying' because it might be worth hanging on if there was a few pennies. We'd always buy sweets with the pennies on our way home to Cabra.'

School photograph of Joe Coffey

Vera, Barbara and Kathleen Burke pose for their school photograph. Children from the same family were often grouped together in a school photograph to save their parent's money. One photograph cost one shilling, two cost one shilling and six pennies and three cost two shillings.

Sister Mary Oliver and her class of young boys.

Saint Finbarr's school in Cabra West first opened its doors to boys in 1943. The teacher's tearoom is on the left and the headmaster's office is on the right as you walk in the main door of the school. Most young boys came here from Saint Catherine's school. One teacher in particular kept a set of boxing gloves in the classroom press. When two boys would misbehave he'd have them fight each other in front of the rest of the boys.

'I went to Finbarr's School and was in Mister Gough's class. I never saw a mean streak in him and even when we used to hide or break his cane, he would just pick a pupil to go down to the far shops to buy another one. As I recall they where sixpence each'.

Father O' Farrell and young boys from Saint Finbarr's School

Tony O'Reilly from 75 Fassaugh Avenue, second left.

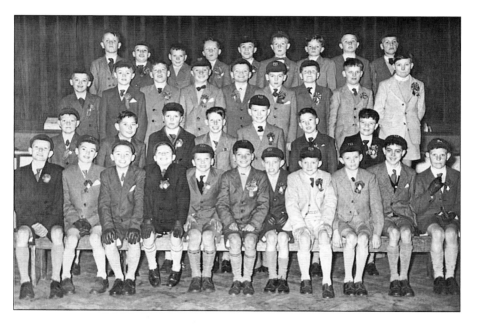

Boy's Confirmation group from Saint Finbarr's School. An average class could have upwards of forty boys in each.

Saint Peter's School in Phibsboro'.

Pupils from Saint Peter's School 1959.

Christ the King School boys entrance.

Christ the King, Cabra National School opened in 1934.

The Cabra Technical School

'I was twelve when I first went mitching. We used to go up to the fields near the canal looking for bird's nests. We wouldn't harm the birds or anything like that. We'd go and look in at the little scaldies and that. There used to be football pitches up there. Then we'd be on the railway. There's one railway that goes up Broombridge and then there's the other one that used to turn down by the playground. I got chased on the railway a few times. There is a long tunnel there at the back of Bachelors factory and there used to be an old railway detective that was on the prowl. There used to be a big 'Culchie' fella there, the railway detective or something he was called. We'd be on one side and he'd see you up on the bank. "Come here boys, no you're not in trouble. Come over". He was waiting to catch you. There used to be a box at the side of the railway carriage and we were told that's where the trolley wheels are kept, you know for making the trolleys. We used to be down looking for them. We went down the railway but mostly up the fields and up around the baths and the dump. We used to hide our schoolbags in the hedges up at the fields. Then we used to just ramble back and wait near the school until the kids were coming out and go home'.

Chapter 10

Religious Occasions

Cabra West officially became a parish in 1946. Originally Cabra West had no church of its own. Some families attended Mass in the nearby chapel in St Joseph's School for deaf children on Rathoath Road. Other families travelled to Old Cabra and Phibsborough while others chose to walk into town to the Pro-Cathedral for Mass. In 1946 the parish priest Canon Valentine Burke was determined that Cabra West should have a church of its own. In December of 1953 the Church of the Most Precious Blood was blessed and officially opened on the eve of the Marion Year at a cost of £100,000 with £7 per day in interest paid to the bank. The Archbishop of Dublin and Primate of all Ireland the Most Rev. J.C. Mc Quaid D.D. blessed the foundation stone and foundations. His Grace gave generous donations towards the building. Rev. Father Kilcullen, a Salesian Father originally from Killala Road and the first to be ordained from the parish celebrated the first Mass.

The Church of the Most Precious Blood.

The High Altar and Communion rails were gifted to the church by Mr Patrick Barrett. The side altars were donated by the Sacred Heart sodalities. Other generous donors included Mr Daniel Dowling, Mr John Geoghegan, Mr William Lucas and Mrs Reid. Many parishioners both young and old also contributed to the building fund. The church was built in a modern Romanesque style and has seating in the nave for 1,700 people. The gallery is capable of seating 300 people. On each side of the nave there are shrines and confessionals. There are large sacristies, a Lady Chapel, store rooms, a baptistery and also a mortuary next to the priest's sacristy. The altars and altar rails are in carved selected marbles. The side altars have carved oak canopies and the tabernacle is in bronze. A model of the proposed church was made by Mr Patrick St. Ledger of Rathoath Road. The original tin church was moved to Terenure parish.

The Evening Standard Newspaper 1953.

'In a now thickly populated part of Dublin, once a wild wooded place, workmen are finishing this week one of the finest new churches to be built in the city in recent years. The new Church of the Precious Blood, West Cabra will be blessed on Sunday, on the eve of the opening of the great Marian Year. His Grace, the Archbishop of Dublin and Primate of Ireland, Most Rev. John Charles Mc Quaid, D.D. who blessed the foundation stone and foundations will perform Sunday's ceremony. It will be followed later the same day with the opening of a Triduum for the Marian Year at which Rev J.C. Moloney S.J., Belvedere College, will preach. On that day Mass will be said for the last time in the temporary iron chapel which was formely part of the College of St. Columban, Dalgan Park, Navan, by Very Rev. V. Burke P.P. The new high altar and communion rails have been the gift of Mr. Patrick Barrett. Other generous donors include Mr. Daniel Dowling, Mr. John Geoghegan, Mr. William Lucas,

The old tin church in Sean Mc Dermot Street.

Mrs Reid and many others. The woodblock flooring was supplied and fitted by Dwyer & Daly Ltd, 16 Nth. Great George's Street. The old tin church is about to be transferred to Templeogue. Mr. John E. McGetrick was the foreman in charge of the building. It is hoped to provide an organ within the next year. Over the main entrance is a representation of the Chalice and Host with Angels in adoration carved out of Portland Stone. This is the work of two brothers, Albert and Oliver Power, stonemasons. The front elevation is completed with a 130 feet high bell tower'.

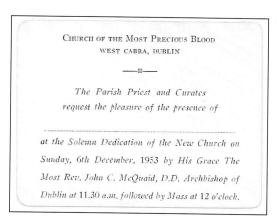

CHURCH OF THE MOST PRECIOUS BLOOD
WEST CABRA, DUBLIN

The Parish Priest and Curates
request the pleasure of the presence of

at the Solemn Dedication of the New Church on
Sunday, 6th December, 1953 by His Grace The
Most Rev. John C. McQuaid, D.D. Archbishop of
Dublin at 11.30 a.m. followed by Mass at 12 o'clock.

Invitation to the dedication of the Church of
The Most Precious Blood 6th December 1953.

The May Procession on Killala Road 1960s.

Crowds attending Mass on Drumcliffe Road.

The May Procession 1965.

Mass being celebrated in the Dominican Convent School.

A Cabra Scout group marching on parade along Killala Road.

Local men and altar boys with Canon Burke.

The Armed Forces providing a guard of honour for the Corpus Christi procession.

Altar boys at the Dominican Convent School.

Our Lady's statue on Quarry Road.

The May altar in the compound on Drumcliffe Road.

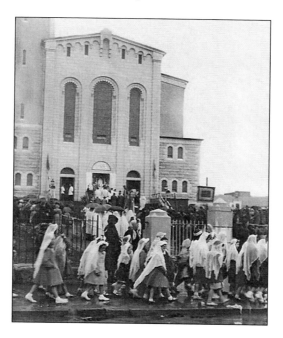

Young girls wearing their veils as they walk into the Church.

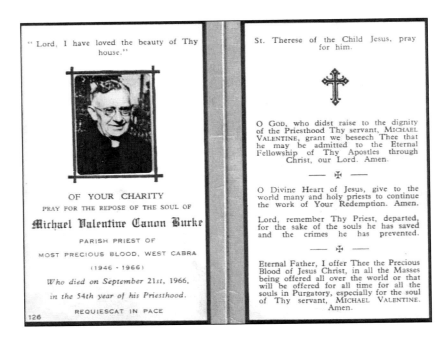

"Lord, I have loved the beauty of Thy house."

OF YOUR CHARITY

PRAY FOR THE REPOSE OF THE SOUL OF

Michael Valentine Canon Burke

PARISH PRIEST OF

MOST PRECIOUS BLOOD, WEST CABRA

(1946 - 1966)

Who died on September 21st, 1966,

in the 54th year of his Priesthood.

REQUIESCAT IN PACE

126

St. Therese of the Child Jesus, pray for him.

O GOD, who didst raise to the dignity of the Priesthood Thy servant, MICHAEL VALENTINE, grant we beseech Thee that he may be admitted to the Eternal Fellowship of Thy Apostles through Christ, our Lord. Amen.

O Divine Heart of Jesus, give to the world many and holy priests to continue the work of Your Redemption. Amen.

Lord, remember Thy Priest, departed, for the sake of the souls he has saved and the crimes he has prevented.

Eternal Father, I offer Thee the Precious Blood of Jesus Christ, in all the Masses being offered all over the world or that will be offered for all time for all the souls in Purgatory, especially for the soul of Thy servant, MICHAEL VALENTINE. Amen.

The Very Rev. Valentine Burke P.P.

An open-air altar set up in the inner city.

Religious processions were always very solemn occasions.

The Eucharistic Congress 1932.

CERTIFICATE OF BAPTISM

I certify that according to the Baptismal register of this Parish.

Name ____ Martin Coffey.

Born on ____ 31st Oct 1951

was Baptised according to the Rites of the Holy Catholic Church

on ____ 9th Nov 1951.

Parents ____ Bernard Coffey + Mary Spellman.

Sponsors ____ Margaret O Brien.

Confirmed ____ 28th March 1963.

Married ____ no entry in record.

Signed ____ M Mooney ____ Date ____

Here is a copy of a Baptismal Certificate from the parish of the Precious Blood, Cabra West. The certificate clearly states the full name of the child and the correct birth date. The date on which the baptism took place is also indicated along with the names of both parents. The mother's maiden name was given along with the name of any sponsors or godparents. Also mentioned on the baptismal certificate is the date that the child made his or her Confirmation and where applicable a marriage date. These records are stored in the Church and kept up to date in many instances by the parish clerk.

Procession in Sean Mc Dermot Street.

St Peter's Church Phibsboro'

Our Lady's Grotto in Cabra West.

Coffey girls and Kathleen Cullivan 34 Killala Road.

'The only memory I have of my First Holy Communion is going around the houses on Killala Road and Mrs. Quinlan gave me a shilling. That's the only memory I have of that. One other memory is of me Da bringing me to see his relations. We were walking up a street and there was a railway bridge over it. My Da was lighting a cigarette and I reached out to hold his hand. A woman passing by said 'don't you start smoking, you won't grow'. I was putting up my hand to grab his hand to walk along the street and he was lighting a cigarette at the same time. That's the only memory I have of my First Holy Communion. I remember being in the flats in Sheriff Street and they were all pulling out of me. 'Give's a look at your frilly knickers and give's a look at your dress and how much have you got in your bag'. I can't really remember much more of my Communion for some reason'.

Our Lady's statue on Saint Attracta Road.

The Church of Christ the King in Cabra.

Chapter 11

Weddings

Bridie Malone on her wedding day in 1957 with a line-up of the 'Royalettes' the famous dance troupe from the Theatre Royal which she was a part.

Jim & Carmel Cleary and neighbours at a Dingle Road Wedding.

Eileen Hayes from lower Killala Road marries Martin Branagan from lower Carnlough Road 30th July 1959.

Tom O'Reilly and Elizabeth Walsh 75 Fassaugh Avenue on their wedding day. L-R: Hugh, Laurence and Leo O'Reilly. The lady on the right is Marie Walsh and the young girl in front of her is Marie Wolahan from Fassaugh Avenue.

Martin & Eileen Branagan wedding group 1959.

Tony Duffy from Inchicore marries Chris Coffey from Killala
Road, Cabra West 1963.

Nellie and Jimmy Nolan wedding in Cabra West 1959.

Paddy (Danny) Mitchell and Francis Dunne wedding.

Peter Mooney and May Moore wedding.

Scally Wedding 1959.

Horst Hentschel marries Bridie Malone 1957. Horst was a saxophone and clarinet player. He performed with Mick Delahunty and his band and also with the Paddy Kearns Band.

Edward Dean and Bridgid L'Estrange wedding day in 1970 with her parents Michael and Margaret, her sister Rita and brothers Phil and Alan.

Paddy Hayes and Martin Branagan 1959.

Martin Branagan and Eileen Hayes signing the marriage register in the presence of Father 'Flash' Kavanagh.

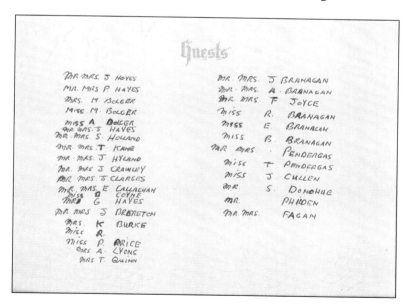

Martin & Eileen's Wedding Guest List.

Wedding guests arrive at the Church of
the Most Precious Blood, Cabra West.

Paddy and Fran Mitchell on their wedding day.

Warm congratulations to the bride and groom,
Bridie Malone and Horst Hentschel from the people of Cabra.

A happy day for the Hayes family.

Horst Hentschel from Germany with his new bride Bridie Malone
and Father Kavanagh 1957

Noel Jordan, Annamoe Drive & Kitty Rodden, Carnlough Road.

Patty Lynch 90 Drumcliffe Road and Gerry Kavanagh
from Fourth Road in East Wall on their wedding day.

Chapter 12

Music and Entertainment

Finbarr's Hall 1957

Back row: left-right: Alan L'Estrange, Drummer: Sean Brown, right: Dermot Mc Evoy. **Second from back row:** Jimmy Farrelly, Terry Dillon, Larry Maguire & Andy Reddy. **Third from back row:** left: Liam Donnelly, third from left: Paul Tormey, fourth from left: Larry Moore. **Front row:** fifth from left: Denny Wilders and Conductor: Stephen Moore.

'My name is Alan L'Estrange and I came from Killala Road in Cabra West. In the 1950s I played with the Cabra West Accordion Boy's Band which was run by Jim Brown from Carnlough Road. We had our practice sessions in his house so you can imagine how tight that was but we didn't know any better. The smaller group was the original band and that was in 1956. The bigger group was about 1957 and both photos were taken in Finbarr's Hall as we used to play there a lot at variety shows which were very popular as there was no television. We also played in other halls all around Dublin and sometimes during the intervals in dance halls in town'.

Cabra West Accordion Band 1956

Back row: Alan L'Estrange, left, Drummer: Gene Stirrat, second left, Andy Bannon, Singer, Stephen Moore, right. **Front row:** Tommy Monahan, second from left, Conductor: Jackie Burke, Michael Mahon, fifth from left, Andy Reddy, right, Kevin Mahon.

Cabra West Accordion Band 1957

Members of the Boys' Accordion Band

The Creoles band with Willie Lynch on bass guitar.

Ballroom Dance champions Barbara Burke, back row left, with
Helen Coffey, centre and Breda Burke front right.

Two more Cabra West bands.

The Chimes Band with Ian Stirrat

The Blue Diamonds.

Dickie Rock and the Blue Clavons
John, Gerry and Harry Hardy are from Swilly Road.
Harry Hardy worked in Williams & Woods Ltd. where many
young people from Cabra West were employed.

The lead drummer is Mr. O'Neill from
140 Lower Carnlough Road.

Martin Coffey 1960's.

Sonny Parker as Al Jolson singing his heart
out at the Cabra Grand talent competition

Dickie Rock from Dingle Road went on to become famous with
the Miami Showband from 1963 to 1977. He represented Ireland
in the Eurovision Song Contest in 1966. He had twenty five Irish
hits in twenty years and eight top ten hits.

Rita Malone, Bridie Malone and Pat Conway

The Theatre Royal was situated in Hawkins Street and was opened in 1935. It had a seating capacity for 3,700 people. As many as 300 people were allowed to stand. It was used as both a theatre and a cinema. The theatre also had a fine restaurant. Jimmy Campbell conducted the 25-piece resident orchestra. There was also a troupe of singer-dancers called the Royalettes. Many famous household names appeared on the stage over the years. Jimmy O'Dea along with Maureen Potter, Cecil Sheridan, Jack Cruise and Noel Purcell kept audiences entertained for many years. Judy Garland had a sell-out performance in 1951. Some of the big stars to appear were Gracie Fields and Jimmy 'The Nose' Durante. Cabra West also had its talent on the stage of the Theatre Royal. Bridie Malone and her sister Rita were members of the Royalettes. Due to rising costs and the popularity of the cinema, the Theatre Royal eventually closed its doors on the 30th June 1960.

'My grandmother was Molly Malone from 52 Liscannor Rd.
I think she was quite a character and well known throughout
Cabra. My mother is Bridie Malone and also a lot of people knew
her because she was one of the Royalettes in the 1950's. Her
younger sister Rita was also a Royalette. I never lived in Cabra
but I sure spent a lot of time there visiting my grandparents. I lived
in Blanchardstown - but I did attend the Cabra Convent for 2
years (1969 and 1970) before we moved to Germany'.

Ingrid Mary Schneider

The State Cinema Phibsboro'

'You had Hopalong Cassidy, you had Lash Laroo and you had Whip Wilson all the cowboys that were out there. You had a thing that they used to have on Saturday mornings, a 'Follow Upper' and maybe Batman and Robin type of things. This week they'd be trapped in a car or in a lorry for transporting money and it'd go over the cliff with them in it. 'Come next week' the voice would say 'see what happens next'. 'Ah Jaysus they're gone over the cliff. They're dead'. So you'd go next week. And just as they are getting to the cliff they jump out. You've already seen them going over the cliff. Next week before they get to the cliff they jump out. They were great, pure innocence. In later years I used to go to the pictures Monday, Friday and Sunday. You'd go three times a week. If you didn't book your seats for Sunday night you probably wouldn't get in. The picture houses used to be packed. There were people who used to have their own seats; they used to kind of call them that. Every week you paid for your two seats or for your four seats, whatever it was. They were your seats. You got them week in and week out. You would go over maybe on a Wednesday or a Thursday and get them. Then maybe on a Friday night you would go in, people who didn't have their own seats went in and booked a seat on a Friday for Sunday. Or if you were well known say or if you hadn't collected your seats by Thursday they would let them go on Friday'.

The Plaza Cinerama, formerly the Plaza Cinema, in Parnell Street.

The Catholic Temperance Club Parnell Square

The Broadway Cinema Manor Street

The Broadway Cinema in Manor Street originally opened in 1914 as the Manor Cinema showing silent films. It eventually closed in 1956. It had a seating capacity for 630 patrons. The Broadway originally opened up as the Manor Cinema and then changed to the Palladium and eventually to the Broadway. One of the first films to be shown in the Manor Cinema was a 1918 silent film called 'He Comes Up Smiling' starring Douglas Fairbanks. With silent films background music was usually supplied by a pianist or a small orchestra. In the Manor Cinema the manageress Miss Lily Fagan, played the piano while her sister played the cello and there was also a violinist making up a musical trio. The cinema was open seven days a week with three shows and a matinee every Sunday. Children paid four pence admission and adults paid nine pence. There were children's' competitions with singing and dancing. Jimmy O'Dea from the Theatre Royal performed there and Paddy Crosbie performed his 'School around the Corner' there also. Robert Hartney was one of the longest employed ushers in the cinema. He retired when it closed in 1956.

The Cinerama in Talbot Street

'We went to the Broadway down in Manor Street when you'd get sixpence off your Ma[or Da. You'd go down to Manor Street and it was four pennies into the pictures and that left you with two pennies to spend. Sometimes we'd get the bus down which was a penny. But you never got the bus back. You bought two pennies worth of sweets and you'd walk home. It was a big cinema and it was four pennies for the seats down stairs and six pennies for the seats upstairs. There would be a queue on the right hand side and on the left hand side. They would let all the four penny seats in first until they were filled up. Then they would let all the six penny ones in up stairs. If there were any seats left upstairs and the six penny queue was gone they would then let the four penny queue sit up at the back upstairs. The toilet was halfway down the stairs from the balcony and you had to come down stairs to go to the toilet. If you were down stairs you had to go halfway up. Rather than go down stairs the boys would pee on the floor'.

The Cabra Grand on Quarry Road.

'I remember the Cabra Grand being built but I can't remember the year. I do remember when it was 8 pence to go on a Sunday to the afternoon matinee. At the time you could go to the Finbarr's Hall for 6 pence but of course it was a big deal to go to the Grand if you could afford it. We used to queue to get in the side door. Later they used to have the midnight matinees and they were great entertainment. There was a stage show before the movie. At the time I was working in Unidare in Finglas and a few of us from work would go together. There was one impersonator that used to do Frank Sinatra to records but I can't remember his name. He really was terrific and very popular. To this day I still associate the smell of popcorn with the Cabra Grand. It was the first time I ever saw it or tasted it. One of the Kelly brothers from Killala Road was the chief usher in the Grand. The first film shown at the Grand was "Sitting Pretty" and starred Clifton Webb and Maureen O'Hara'.

The Palace Theatre Dame Street

The Queens Theatre in Pearse Street.

The Capitol Cinema, Prince's Street.

The Gaiety Theatre, South King Street.

The Plaza Cinema on the corner of
Parnell Street and Dorset Street.

Jim Murphy outside the Theatre Royal
in Hawkins Street shortly before it was pulled down.

Although she was not a Cabra girl Eileen Lalor nee O'Connor was one of the Royalettes who attended the wedding of Bridie Malone and Horst Hentschel. Her sister Philomena Doyle was also in show business.

Eileen Lalor on stage

Royalette girl Eileen Lalor

Chapter 13

Sports and Social

This photograph of Killala United junior soccer team was taken in 1946. The team are Back Row L-R: Ned Donnelly, Tommy Creevy, Christie Rogers, Jimmy Meade, George 'Duke' Kavanagh and Joey Maloney. Front Row L-R: Michael O'Donnell, Mick Mitchell, George Marshall, Tony Doran and Johnnie Sutton. The boy standing in the background on the left of the photograph is Seamus Hayes. The group of boys standing on the right side of the photograph are Jimmy Sherry, Paddy Kealy, Joey Creevy, Alf Marshel and Tommy Rogers is the little boy in short trousers. The lower Killala Road team was run by Mr Courtney, Mr Coffey and Mr Hayes. The men who formed the road leagues had great foresight in forming soccer teams from different age groups and from different roads. It was a great outlet for young boys bursting with energy and most of all it kept them out of mischief. The original team jerseys were probably old rugby shirts. The above lads were so disappointed when they were told that they were only getting togged out for this photograph and had to take the gear off after it was taken.

Killala Road senior team (date unknown, Back row L-R: Sonny Stuart, Joey O'Toole, Paddy O'Donnell, Peter O'Neill, Paddy Hayes and Jimmy Meade. From row L-R: Unknown, Tommy Moore, Joey Creevy, Unknown and Shay Pepper.

Back row L-R: Mr Thomas Courtney, Dermot Nolan, Paddy Hayes, Eddie Mitchell and Paddy Kealy. Front row L-R: Jimmy Meade, Tommy 'the hare' Creevy, Christie Byrne, Bill Courtney and Tom Courtney.

Michael Whelan from Carnlough road played in the Schoolboy International League when Ireland played against Wales in Dalymount Park 1952.

'A story is told that one day after finishing a football game a mother of one of the young players from the Killala Junior soccer team invited all her son's team into her house for a plate of stew. When the boys walked into the kitchen they saw a cat balancing on the edge of the stew pot with its head bent into the pot. The poor cat overbalanced and fell into the hot stew. The good lady of the house caught the cat by the scruff of the neck, gave it a shake over the pot and flung it down the hallway and out through the front door. She then had the young lads sit around her table and served each one up a plate of hot stew'.

Bohemians' football teams.

John Bracken with his brother and a friend standing beside
Willie Hogan in the Phoenix Park.

This happy lot are part of a supporters group who headed off by bus to Navan to cheer on their local Cabra hurling team.

Liam Whelan's grave in Glasnevin. He played for Manchester United and died in the Munich air disaster of 6th February 1958.

The Cabra Harriers Number One Cross Country Team.
L-R: Jim Murphy Fassaugh Road, Willie Brennan, John Cummins,
Willie Brady, P. Ganna, D. Bernard and Tony Cummins.

Cabra lads on the Finglas Labs Soccer Team.

St Anthony's Boys Club.

This photo shows a young football team from Saint Anthony's Boys Club who at the time may have been based in Eccles Street. The photo was taken over sixty years ago. The names of the young footballers are, front row: John Cummins, his brother Tony Cummins (their mother was a dealer in Moore Street. They lived on Jarleth Road), Sean Doherty from Fassaugh Road...facing the Playground, Jemmers Mc Kendrick and Philip Brady (from Fassaugh Road, beside the Fassaugh Stores). The front row is: Unsure, Jim Murphy, Goalkeeper Buggy, Anthony Scanlon lived two doors away from the Murphy's on Fassaugh Road. His mother was also a dealer in Moore Street, Tierney and Morrissey. Some of these boys came from Saint Attracta Road.

St Anthony's Boys' Club.

Eugene Naughton

'St Anthony's Boys' Club was located in Nelson St, off Eccles Street. The club was run by a group of lay-men known as the Brothers who were a terrific bunch of people giving selflessly of their time and more often than not their money to poor kids from the surrounding areas of the club and from the lower end of Cabra; kids for the most part who didn't have the proverbial seat in their trousers at that time back in the late 1950's. I know of nobody who attended that club all those years ago who doesn't have happy memories of their time spent there. There were seniors and juniors nights but mostly the activities were the same; PT, shuttlecock (before it was Badminton), table tennis, draughts, ludo, twenty questions, (animal, vegetable or mineral!) and sing songs. Then there were arts and crafts where we made purses and wallets. I can still get the smell of the freshly tanned leather we used.

The Postman's Bike

During the summer nights we were brought to the Phoenix Park for outdoor physical training (laps around the polo grounds, sprints and relay running.) Once a year there was a Sports Day competition with other boys clubs in the Ivy Grounds in Crumlin There were lots of glittering prizes (it seemed to me) on offer. And then there was the annual weeks' holiday in Lonan Murphy (?) House in Sallins, Co Kildare. This was one of the grand old big country houses set in its own grounds that ran right down to the Liffey where there was diving platform. The happiest days of my childhood were spent there. Every day was sports day; swimming, football, cricket, cross country running and paper chases. At night ghost stories were told and songs were sung. And who among us at that time can forget Peader Daly from Etna Road singing the songs of the great Little Richard. And then there were the madcap pillow fights late at night, one dormitory against the other. Oh bliss it was to be alive back then and part of all that! The Brothers of St Anthony's Boys Club made all that possible True gentlemen every one of them'.

Chapter 14

Summer Time & Holidays

The open-air baths in Cabra.

A daytrip to the seaside was organised through the newly formed Cabra West Tenants Association. Double decker buses were hired to pick up families from the various roads in the area. A day out to Bray or Bettystown with lots of sandwiches and flasks of tea was a great treat for the family.

The Coffey's in Portmarnock.

The little brown corduroy suits on these boys would have been purchased in the Blackrock clothing shop in Chatham Street and probably paid for with a Providence cheque.

Dollymount Strand where the tide seldom came in.

Dollymount and Bull Island

Eamonn and Liam O' Kelly in Dollymount.

Public swimming in the Tolka River.

Only boys were allowed to swim in the Cabra baths. Girls were encouraged to swim and paddle in the section of the nearby Tolka River known locally as the 'Silver Spoon'. The Tolka River is situated behind the wire fence on the right side of the photograph. It was from this river that the water for the swimming pool was taken. To the left of the photograph there was a long continues wall with a gate at each end. This wall continued around to the area in the foreground of the picture. There was continues seating along the inside of the wall for boys to leave their clothes on when in swimming. The sheltered area housed a pump house and the caretakers shed. There is also a covered area for children to use. The area of the pool nearest to the pump house is where the younger children had to swim and paddle. The older and more experienced boys used the deep end to dive and swim in. The land on the far side of the Tolka River belonged to the Craigie family who were owners of the Merville Dairy on the main Finglas Road. Most every family in Cabra had milk from this dairy delivered to their doorstep each morning. The Craigie family also dealt in cattle and had plenty of dealings with the cattle market in nearby Prussia Street.

Mr & Mrs Bryan with their daughter Elaine
on the beach at Rush, County Dublin.

In Dollymount it was often possible to buy a pot of boiling water
to make your own tea with. The fresh sea air would put a great
appetite on young children and parents alike. Some sandwiches
were filled with soggy tomatoes while others had raw onions or
maybe plain margarine in them. It never mattered to hungry little
mouths. The parent's would often take one bus into city centre and
have the family walk the rest of the way to the beach.

The Sunshine House Balbriggan.

Many young boys and girls from Cabra were sent away for a week's holiday to the Sunshine House in Balbriggan. The children slept in single beds in long dormitories. In 1935 Rochford House was purchased by the St of Vincent de Paul. The original house was used to give underprivileged children from the notorious Dublin slums a week's holiday by the sea. The children were looked after by volunteer men and women. The present building was constructed from 1940-1945, with various improvements carried out over the years. Sunshine House is now a state of the art holiday centre were over 100 boys and girls are taken each week of the summer season. Since its foundation Sunshine House has catered for over 70,000 young children. The children were taken by train from Connolly station in Dublin. This was reminiscent of a scene from a WWII movie showing the children from cities across Britain being evacuated for safe-keeping to the countryside.

Most nights the children were entertained with a film or stage show. In some instances the children themselves provided the entertainment. This little boy has a captivated audience.

A trip to the beach was one of the highlights of a child's time in Balbriggan. Competitions were sometimes held for the best sandcastle built. Each of the boys above was provided with swim wear for the occasion.

These boys obviously brought their own swim wear.

Sunshine House boys building sandcastles in Balbriggan

The stony beach in Bray

Bray Head and seafront.

People often climbed to the top of Bray Head and stood at the cross there to admire the view of Dublin Bay in one direction and Greystones Beach in the other. A rail car was originally situated at the foot of the Head that would carry people up some of the way. To most families from Cabra, Bray was most famous for its amusement arcades and Candy Floss.

Rosanna Crowe Broombridge and Betty O'Neill in Wexford 1954.

'The Ma' brought us up to a fruit fields just up off Cardiffbridge down Scribblestown Lane, right down to the end of it. We used to pick the fruit down there. I remember doing that a few times. That's when there were a few cottages there on the left hand side going up to Cardiffbridge. People were living in them then. It was another world there and then, another time'.

This photograph of Cabra Ladies was taken in Glendalough, Co. Wicklow. In the picture are: front row l-r: Mrs Grimes & daughter Marjorie, 89 Drumcliffe Road, Mrs Lanton & daughter? Mrs Lynch 90 Drumcliffe Road, Elsie McDonald from town and Mrs Callen 83 Drumcliffe Road. Back row? --Katie Callen, ? Doyle Carnlough Road, Molly Malone behind Mrs Lynch, and Kay Brannigan who worked with Mrs Lynch in the laundry.

Anna and Joan Donovan from Drumcliffe Drive Cabra West.

Chapter 15

Houses & Shops of Yesterday and Today

This house on Carnlough Road is waiting to be demolished.

'When we first moved into Cabra the house seemed like a Palace, it seemed huge. The kitchen was at one end of the room, it was a sort of a living room. We had the sink and the cooker at one end and the draining board. Then in the corner there was the Coal Hole and if you wanted to blow your nose you had to go into the Coal Hole because my Dad wouldn't let you blow your nose at the table. There was a little porch leading out into the back garden. There was a corner cupboard at the fireplace end. We had a table and a couple of old chairs around the table. The old kitchen dresser came later. We used to drink out of jam jars because we didn't have enough cups'.

Rathoath Road

Some of the houses had walls at the front.

Other houses had railings.

Killala Road and compound

'In one house in particular they had no inside doors and every second step on their stairs was missing. They all went into the fire during the winter'.

Drumcliffe Road and compound.

Killala Road with buntings on display.

'Across the road from our house lived a family and we were terrified of their father. He was a big man and when he was drunk he would strangle one of his chickens and throw it through the front window of his house. He wore a Fedora hat and when he was drunk the hat was always worn upside down'.

Killala Road awaits the Pope's visit.

Annamoe Shops

Shoe Repair Shop

The Cabra Road leading to the Navan Road.

The Old Soldier's Houses on Quarry Road.

Prescott's cleaners and dyers.

Drumcliffe Road

Carnlough Road and Fassaugh Avenue Crossroads.

Another view of Carnlough Road
and Fassaugh Avenue Crossroads.

Strolling past the church on Fassaugh Avenue.

The Old Post Office, originally Hunt's Butchers' shop.

Fassaugh Road

Ventry Park Playground

Rathoath Road

Boland's Corner at Annamoe.

Reid's shop on the Cabra Road.

The Drapery Shop

Shops on the Cabra Road 1951

95A J Mc Keown Hairdressers

97 The Cuala Milk Bar

99 Albert Stein Pork Butchers

99A G Downey

103A John L'Estrange Victuallers

105 The Monument Creamery

105A Frank Speidel Pork Butchers

107 James Cullen Grocers and Provisions Merchant

Clarke's bakery on the Cabra Road

Shops on the Cabra Road 1951

109 J Maguire MPSI Chemists

111 J Doran

113 J. Fahey

115 G. Reid and Son Grocer

117 J. Smith

119 Mrs Flusk

121 Mrs M. Schmutz

123 Richard Dale

Rathoath Road

A row of shops on Fassaugh Avenue.

The old Capitol Stores

In 1951 the shops on Fassaugh Avenue is listed as follows:

Christ the King Food Centre,
12 M. Whelan Wine Merchant
22 J. Finley Grocery and Provision
24 Mc Gee & Laverty Victuallers
26 Pelly Chemists
28 P Turner
30 P O'Gorman
32 Peter Kennedy Ltd bakers & Confectioners
32 J. Melvin Groceries
56 T. Hunt Victuallers
58 T.A. Beechinor Town Sub Post Office
60 J. Brady Erin Café
68 William & Company
70 Boland's Bakers & Confectioners
70 Doctor Watson
72 P. Barrett Capitol Stores

Fassaugh Avenue

There were also shops situated on Fassaugh Road and the Cabra Road area, including Annamoe. Some people opened up smaller shop type facilities in their own homes or in a van parked outside their house. It wasn't unusual for someone to sell goods from their front parlour window. One woman on Killala Road sold broken seaside rock from her parlour window that was stored under her mattress. These shop type premises sold everything from cigarettes to bread to potatoes and the newspaper. Granny Groves from lower Killala Road delivered newspapers door to door to most houses in Cabra West. Mister Groves had a newspaper stand outside Eason's Bookstore in O'Connell Street. Young boys were often grafted in by Granny Groves to help her with the deliveries. They were always paid a few bob on Saturday and at Christmas time there was always a party given in the Grove's house for all the little helpers.

Matt Whelan's pub was built on what was originally known as Lyon's Hill. Nearby a turf depot and a shed for the Corporation men was built. Many young boys such as John Burke from Broombridge collected and delivered turf for the elderly of the parish. Any money John earned on the deliveries he donated to the Old Folks Christmas party.

Cabra cottages on the Navan Road.

The Yellow Dairy was situated on the Old Cabra Road where this service station stands today. One day as the cattle men were trying to persuade a bull to climb on board a cattle truck it broke loose from its chains and ran down the road towards the cattle market.

Jim Murphy at his parent's home on Fassaugh Road

Phibsboro'

Fassaugh Avenue shops and church.

The shopping areas of Cabra became a great focal point for people to meet each other on a daily basis. Shopping took on a particular ritual for families and more especially the mother of the home. By ten o'clock most mornings the shops were filled to overflowing as people queued for their meat, vegetables and other groceries. Fassaugh Avenue had two sets of shops positioned on either side of the church. The smallest shop on Fassaugh Avenue was known as the Chipper Window and it was the only shop you couldn't walk into. It had a serving hatch through which customers gave their orders and received their goods i.e. cigarettes, sweets, minerals or ice cream. The ice cream was sold in a block or in wafers. The wafers came in two sizes, small or large. The small wafer cost three old pennies and the large wafer cost six old pennies. Fassaugh Avenue began at Quarry Road and ended at Rathoath Road. The two main shops on Quarry Road were 181 Mrs Reid's Post Office and 183 Mrs Massey's Grocers.

The remains of a cottage at Cardiffbridge near Cabra.

The Deegan's bungalow on Broombridge Road.

Chapter 16

A Selection of Family Names from 1951

Annamoe Drive

1 P Rooney,   3 F Duffy,   5 R Smith,   7 J Kelly

9 Wm Norton   11 E Behan   13 P O'Reilly   15 James Dunne

17 T Nevin   19 N Ryan   21 J Mc Keever   23 John Kelly

Annamoe Parade

1 Frawley   2 Smith   3 Michael Bermingham

Annamoe Terrace

25A Mrs O'Reilly…Grocer   26 Provisions Merchant

27 Newman   28 Quinn Grocers   29 O' Malley

30 Myles   31 Kavanagh   36 Byrne   37 Grimes

38 Reynolds   39 Rooney   40 Simpson   41 Thorpe

91 Malone   91A Lawlor   92 Donegan   93 Cafolla's Café

94 Ward   95 Hayes   96 Boland's Ltd Confectioner's phone 41204

Annamoe Road

1 Mc Loughlin Sub Post Office

1A Mc Lennon & Co Undertakers Suppliers

2 Robinson   3 Murray   4 Gaven   5 Gaven   6 Mundow

7 Quinn   8 – 16 Mc Gauren Annamoe Garage   17 Mc Cabe

18 O'Leary   19 Higgins   20 Kelly   21 O'Rourke   22 Whelan

23 Burke   24 O' Farrell   25 Murnane   26 Kelly   27 Burke

28   Kane   29 O' Connell   30 Tully

Cabra Road

4 Mrs J Telford Confectionary   8 Russell   10 Farrelly Victuallers

12 Cuffe & Son Cattle Salesmen   14 – 30 Cuffe's Cattle Lairs

32 Annamoe garage

J H Keogh Cabra Cottage   Mrs Quirke Poplar Lodge

J Kavanagh Cabra Villas   P Mooney Cabra Lodge

110 Shelby   112Maloney   114 Dunne   116 Drennan

118 Capt Lawless   120 Fitzgerald

122 Blanche McGrath M.C.H.S.

Bannow Road

1 Mrs B Mooney   3 J Traynor   5 S O'Callaghan   7 G Hapgood

9 Mrs M Keogh   11 C Kearns   13 Mrs M Denny   15 M Grogan

17 P Dunne   19 P Kelly   21 J Burke   23 Thomas Logan

25 J Givens   27 L Mooney   29 Mrs Thompson

31 Thos Mc Donald   33 Mrs E Coughlan   35 Mrs Fanning

37 Mrs I Jevers   39 P Hogan   41 J Lariney   43 Chris' Medden

45 Mrs Keegan   47 J O'Dowd   49 Teresa Sheridan

51 Mr M Roper   53 David Brazier   55 Stephen Swords

57 Mrs E Fay   59 William Deaton   61 M Fallon

63 H Byrne   65 Mrs E Dillon

Kilkiernan Road

1 F Donaghy   3 J Glynn   5 Mrs E Cooke   7 Wm Lithedder

9 W Duffy   11 M Murphy   13 J Masterson   15 J Kinneally

17 P Walsh   19 W Kelly   21 F Walters   23 M Grogan

25 Sloan   27 Kavanagh   29 Farrell   31 Spence   33 Davidson

35 Finnegan   37 Malone   39 Thomas Dunne   41 Butler

43 Donlan   45 Bradshaw   47 Martin   49 Bryan   51 Tracey

53 Mullins   55 Williams   57 Mc Evoy   59 Neill   61 Rogers

63 Brennan   65 Bergin

122 Reilly   124 Clinton   126 Trimble   128 Flynn   130 Hughes

132 Nelson   134 Kelly   134A Rent Office   136 Weir

2 Geoghegan   4 Mc Dowell   6 Dee   8 Fleming   10 O'Gorman

12 Ward   14 Reid   16 Heasley   18 O' Hanlon   20 Mc Cann

22 Mc Cabe   24 Butler   26 Costigan   St Finbarr's School

Killala Road Lower (1-113)

1 Mitchell   3 Bergin   5 Kiely   7 King   9 Moran   11 Abbott

13 Byrne   15 O' Hanlon   17 Quinn   19 Crawley   21 Hayes

23 Sherwood   25 Callaghan   27 Doran   29 Lally   31 Wade

33 Keegan   35 Kemple   37 Moloney   39 Byrne   41 Carney

43 Farrell   45 Wm Barry   47 Mc Donald   49 Rabbit

51 Bolger   53 Brendan Flanagan   55 Hensey   57 Norton

59 Sullivan   61 Groves   63 Leetham   65 Deegan   67 Kelly

69 Mc Carthy   71 Mc Guinness   73 Grant   75 Slater   77 Smith

79 Byrne   81 Flaherty   83 Mc Mahon   85 Kelly   87 Mc Kenna

89 Spain   91 Lynch   93 Hogan   95 O' Donovan   97 Paget

99 Hurley   101 Caffrey   103 Swords   105 Amos   107 Flood

109 Kelly   111 Garland   113 Walsh

Lower Killala Road (2 – 156)

2 J O'Toole 4 J Mc Keever 6 M Pepper 8 A Marshall

10 M Purdue 12 P Stewart 14 P Hammond 16 P O'Gorman

18 P Malone 20 J Crainey 22 T Rogers 24 W Nolan

26 M Meade 28 J Hamilton 30 S Quinlan 32 M Barry

34 K O'Brien 36 B Coffey 38 C Quinn 40 M Kavanagh

42 M Wyatt 44 E O'Donnell 46 J Carey 48 J Slattery

50 R Duggan 52 R Upton 54 J Mc Quaid 56 T Ashton

58 D Bradley 60 W Sherry 62 P Geoghegan 64 S Bowler

66 M Tuohy 68 H Downes 70 J Merton 72 J Taylor

74 C Byrne 76 J Hanley 78 J Kilcullen 80 T Courtney

82 L Mc Namara 84 R Bedford 86 M L'Estrange

88 M Lynch 90 F Mooney 92 W Mooney 94 Mrs Valentine

96 P O'Hanlon 98 R Keenan 100 T Casey 102 T O'Shea

104 J Brogan 106 J Farrell 108 J Murray 110 J Doyle

112 C Leech 114 K Wade 116 K Caird 118 M Crowther

120 C Quinlan 122 C Satelle 124 S Maguire 126 T Mc Cann

128 J Butterly 130 T Keagan 132 D Murphy 134 W Clarke

136 J Brown 138 F Caffrey 140 M Malone

Leix Road

1 Field   3 Murphy   5 Rogers   7 Cahill   9 Nolan

11 Sherlock   13 Hanlon   15 Clancy   17 Byrne   19 Tyrell

21 Hughes   23 Connolly   25 Morgan   27 Kennedy

29 Boyne   31 Keegan

Quarry Road

50 The Homestead Wine & Spirits   52 Meehan Snowville

54 Brady Victuallers   56 Peter Kennedy Baker and Confectioner

58 Dr Davis   60 The Cabra Grand Cinema

62 Murtagh Sweets and Tobacco   64 O' Sullivan   66 O' Neill

Broombridge Road

2 Nolan   4 Guiney   6 Slattery   8 Brady   10 Walsh   12 Hayes

14 Rogers   16 Gilligan   18 Kavanagh   20 Copeland

22 Kavanagh   24 Melia   26 Kennedy   28 O' Brien   30 Deegan

32 Donnelly   34 Long   36 Maguire   38 – 48 Turf Depot

21 Crowe   23 Dillon   25 Robinson   27 Darcey   29 Roche

31 Murray   33 Mc Namara   35 Sheehan   37 Daly   39 Smith

41 Kennedy   43 Lytton   45 Cunningham   47 Sweeney

49 Smith   51 Henshaw

Dingle Road

1 Murray   3 O' Reilly   5 O' Brien   7 Kellehan   9 Corcoran

11 O' Toole   13 Gibney   15 Molloy   17 T Cronin

19 Murney   21 Byrne   23 Hearne

91 Lyons   93 Ruth   95 Daniels

97 O' Neill   99 Molloy   101 Duffy   103 Fulham

105 Charles Mc Carthy   107 Meates   109 Moans

111 O' Reilly   113 Brady   115 Flynn   117 Bracken

119 Daly   121 Bennett   123 Dillon

50 Sherlock   52 Mooney   54 Mulroy   56 Edwards

58 Stone   60 Matthews   62 Owens   64 Mongey

66 Rock   68 Kavanagh   70 Kelly   110 Lee   112 Quinn

114 Haines   116 Dunne   118 Mc Grath   120 Ivory

Inver Road

1 Daly   3 Mc Guire   5 Ledwidge   7 Clarke   9 King

11 Bryan   13 Corrigan   15 Cullen   17 Maher   19 Kelly

21 Mc Elligott   23 Radburn   25 Mc Keever   27 O' Brien

29 Harrop   31 Devers   33 O' Malley   35 Forde

37 O' Brien   39 Kelly   41 Glynn   43 Creevey

45 Cranks   47 Donoghue   49 Barron   51 Mc Donnell

53 Gerathy   55 O' Brien   57 Coote

6 O' Neill   8 Farrell   10 Fay   12 Mc Cabe

14 Murphy   16 O' Rourke   18 Murphy   20 Muldoon

22 Kelly   24 Mc Donald   26 Mc Cudden   28 Lally

30 Thunder   32 Walls   34 Carroll   36 Molloy

38 Aungier   40 Nolan   42 Molomey   44 Hicks

46 Byrne   48 O' Dwyer   50 Reddin   52 Kavanagh

54 Murphy   56 Cullen   58 Donnelly   60 Wylie

Dunmanus Road

1 Campbell   3 Lonergan   5 Morrissey   7 Lynch

9 Somers   11 O' Meara   13 Flynn   15 Allen   17 Owens

19 O' Brien   21 Cooke   23 Duffy

97 Morrissey   99 Evender   101 Cullen   103 Clarke

105 Clancy   107 Parker   109 Kearney   111 Tuohy

113 Cooney   115 Murney   117 Butler   119 Clancy

2 Smith   4 Finn   6 Harris   8 Dignam   10 Kelly

12 Hyland   14 Kavanagh   16 Browne   18 Green   20 Costello

Liscannor Road

1 Tierney   3 O' Reilly   5 Malone   7 Kelly   9 Rafferty

11 Mc Dermott   13 Fulham   15 Ryan   17 Mulligan

19 Patrick Moran Music Teacher   21 Mulroy   23 Kane

25 Johnston   27 Patterson   29 Kelly   31 Mc Entee

33 Mulligan   35 Kavanagh   37 Crawford   39 Carr

41 Moore   43 Gibson   45 Kavanagh   47 Moloney

49 Maguire   51 Higgins

2 Maher   4 Mc Cormack   6 Cleary   8 Collins

10 Burrows   12 Neville   14 Cullen   16 Curren   18 Jordan

20 Thorpe   22 Farrelly   24 Lambert   26 Murphy

28 Mc Elroy   30 Higgins   32 Coughlan   34 Hickey

36 Boyne   38 Dooley   40 Staunton   42 Talbot

44 Bowers   46 Uzell   48 Stewart   50 Murphy   52 Malone

Ventry Drive

1 Flynn   3 Kelly   5 Delaney   7 Flanagan

9 Rowentree   11 Hagan   13 Doyle   15 Uzell

17 Vacant

Ventry Drive

2 Bailey   4 Goddard   6 Gilligan   8 Leonard   10 Finnegan

12 Mulhall   14 O' Brien   16 O' Neill   18 Cavendish

Ventry Park

2 Hill   4 Donnelly   6 Fitzgerald   8 O' Callaghan

10 D'Arcey   12 Hughes   14 Keane   16 Gordon

18 Mc Donald   20 Reid   22 Tyrrell   24 Connenton

26 Uzell   28 Brennan   30 Redmond   32 Martin

34 Flaherty   36 Norton   38 Holmes   40 Nolan

42 Glynn   44 Delaney

Ventry Road

2 O' Connell   4 Dignam   6 Kelly   8 O' Neill

10 Holmes   12 Clarke   14 O' Gorman   16 Host

18 Hall   20 Conway   22 Dunne   24 Ryan

26 Hanaphy   28 Mc Carthy   30 Browne   32 Mannigan

Saint Peter's School 1951

Headmaster: PJ Walsh, Headmistress: Miss Macken

Rathoath Road

7 Henshaw   9 Brannigan   11 Hanley   13 Murtagh

15 Kinsella   17 Rooney   19 Flanagan   21 Lee

23 O' Kane   25 Mc Carthy   27 Mc Ginley   29 Clarke

31 Hall   33 Leonard   35 Gibbons   37 O' Toole

39 Doyle   41 O' Dowd   43 O' Reilly   45 Flaherty

47 Billings   49 Kinsella   51 Pittman

69 Rogers   71 Smith   73 Brerton   75 Morgan

77 Wogan   79 Drew   81 Doyle   83 Power   85 Mahon

87 Maguire   89 Whelan   91 Keenan   93 Crowley

95 Brennan   97 Wall   99 Kellett

221 P Burke   223 Boyne   225 Mullins   227 Mitchell

229 Kelly   231 Murray

Mc Grath's The Bungalow

267 O' Beirne   269 Byrne   271 Malone   273 O' Connor

275 Wallace   277 Green   279 Laydon   281 Smith

283 Mc Cormack   285 Cummins

Drumcliffe Road

1 Byrne   2 Mc Greery   3 Lynch   4 Lawless

5 Mc Hugh   6 Quinn   7 O' Connell   8 O' Brien

9 Mc Kinley   10 King   11 Reddy   12 O' Reilly

13 Mersier   14 White   15 Murphy   16 Mc Cabe

17 Kelly   18 Power   19 O'Donnell   20 Hibbits

21 King   22 Mc Dowell   23 Harrison   24 Brennan

25 Colgan   26 Donnelly   27 Donohue   28 Losty

29 Ryan   30 Brerton   31 Fogarty   32 Fallon

33 Rice   34 O' Connell   35 Dillon   36 Lang

Drumcliffe Road

70 Brabazon   71 Hardy   72 Lynch   73 Phoenix

74 Finglas   75 Doyle   76 Byrne   77 Flynn

78 Hoban   79 Brien   80 O' Connor   81 Barry

82 Callen   83 O' Reilly   84 Davis   85 O' Reilly

86 Moran   87 Browne   88 Doyle   89 Grimes

90 Lynch   91 Byrne   92 Houlett   93 Leech

94 Tyrrell   95 Walsh   96 Quirke   97 O' Reilly

98 Connolly   99 Peter Diffiley 100 Tuite

Drumcliffe Drive

1 Laurence Maguire   2 R Ryan   3 R Bannerman   4 J Kelly

5 P Sheridan   6 A Mc Loughlin   7 M Mullen   8 James Alford

9 Thomas Kane   10 Christopher Donovan   11 T Reid

12 P Maloney   13 P Masterson   14 J Ryan   15 M Callanan

16 M O' Leary

Mulroy Road

1 Farrell   3 Bowler   5 Currahan   7 Rooney

9 Bateman   11 Warren   13 Jackson   15 Mc Grath

17 Murphy   19 Doyle   21 Fennell   23 Ellis

25 Cuddy   27 Kennedy   29 Morris   31 Lynch

33 Fisher   35 Hayden   37 Stynes   39 Hanbury

41 Kealy   43 Lawrence   45 Russell   47 O' Neill

49 Kelly   51 Heffernan

2 Gains   4 O' Reagan   6 Keane   8 Dowdall

10 Brannigan   12 Holmes   14 Wilson   16 Sheridan

18 Johnston   20 Langan   22 Walsh   24 Reddy

26 Mc Cann   28 Leyden   30 Cummins   32 Devine

34 Garrett   36 Egan   38 Nolan   40 Brazil

42 O' Brien   44 Quinn   46 Gaffney   48 Kennedy

48A Rent Office   50 Butler

Swilly Road

1 Louth   3 O' Keefe   5 Copeland   7 Mc Donnell

9 Murphy   11 Woods   13 Coleton   15 O' Toole

17 Kostick   19 Creevey   21 Delahunty   23 Nolan

25 Dymond   27 Stanley   29 Hanley   31 Kealy

33 Sullivan   35 Smith   37 Corry   39 Slattery

41 Lawless   43 Staunton   45 Ryan   47 Geraghty

49 Mc Kernan   51 Moriarty   53 Mc Fall   55 Keegan

57 Mc Crann   59 King   61 Byrne   63 Kiernan

65 Dennis   67 Donnery   69 Murphy   71 Martin

2 Cullen   4 Shaw   6 Coleton   8 Tierney

10 O' Reilly   12 Cullen   14 Carroll   16 Clarke

18 Keogh   20 Brazil   22 Browne   24 Kelly

26 Purcell   28 King   30 Carroll   32 Mulhall

34 Byrne   36 Hampson   38 Kennedy   40 Murphy

42 Keogh   44 Daly   46 Tucker   48 Kelly

50 Phillips   52 Worn

Fassaugh Avenue

119 Sugg   121 Murphy   123 Lyons   125 Hanley

127 Abbott   129 Morris   131 Mc Elroy   133 Shortt

135 Gibson   137 Whelan   139 Dunne   141 Keogh

143   Paget   145 Brennan   147 Maughan

2 Brophy   2A Whelan   2A J Cruise Grocery and Wine Merchant

4 Griffin   6 Lannigan   8 Foran   10 Power   12 Food Centre

14 Duffy   16 Farrell   18 Abbott   20 Geeling

22 Charles Haite Grocer and Provisions

1 Brady   3 Collins   5 Coleman   7 O' Brien

9 Murphy   11 Dempsey   13 Murphy   15 Leddy

17 Mc Ginnity   19 Christina O' Neill   21 Ayres

23 Carolan   25 Walsh   27 Doherty   29 Kane

103 Germaine   105 Dunne   107 Tormey   109 Simons

111 Donohue   113 Farrelly   115 Lindsey   117 Mc Grattan

Fassaugh Road

30 O' Kelly   32 Scanlon   34 Monaghan   36 Murphy

38 West Stores Grocers   40 Beggsboro House

42 – 44 Hart's Fassaugh Stores   46 Donnelly

48 Brady   50 Donnelly

61 Rooney   63 O' Loughlin   65 Dunne   67 Murphy

69 Jordan   71 Copper   73 Coady   75 Ryan

77 Fannin   79 Gilligan   81 Ryan

Annally Road

1 Kelly   3 King   5 Kelly   7 Foley   9 Malone

11 Woods   13 Cassidy   15 Barrett   17 O' Sullivan

19 Dunne   21 Turner   23 Daly   25 Moloney

27 Nugent   29 Caffrey   31 Hynes

2 Butler   4 Fitzpatrick   6 Smith   8 Kelly   10 Coleman

12 Mc Auley   14 O' Hara   16 Somerville   18 Murphy

20 Martin   22 Murphy

Carnlough Road

1 S Mc Guinness   3 M Kavanagh   5 B Keogh   7 J Early

9 P Flood   11 W Ryan   13 J Cooney   15 E Devine

17 T Kavanagh   19 A Mc Connell   21 J Cullen   23 T Brohoon

25 T Dalton   27 T Brennan   29 J Foy   31 A Doyle

33 T Finnegan   35 J Mc Cann

65 M Montgomery   67 Mrs C Dooly   69 P Canavan   71 F Price

73 M Reddin   75 H Christopher   77 G Farrell   79 J Doyle

81 M Gorman   83 P Morrissey   85 Mrs Marks

109 E O' Connor   111 P Lawlor   113 P Robinson

115 Mrs Mary Flemming   117 J Fahy   119 M Brennan

121 E Mc Mahon   123 J Kinnane   125 T Garrett

127 H Grant   129 D Osborne   131 G Cullen   133 J Branagan

135 J Prendergast   137 C Baker   139 W Anderson

130 Cullen   132 Phelan   134 Cooke   136 O' Driscoll

138 Wilder   140 O' Neill   142 Johnston   144 Cullen

146 Breslin   148 Molloy   150 Stafford

157 Mrs Creamor   159 J Cheevers   161 P O' Neill

163 P Dunne   165 S Scanlon   167 V Lynam

169 Mrs Mary Fallon   171 A Stafford

191 E Mc Ardle   193 S O' Neill   195 H O' Donnell

197 J Foster   199 C Thomas

212 P Dunbar   214 T Fitzpatrick   216 J Gaffney

218 A Abbott   220 M Mc Inerney   222 M Kelly

224 M O' Reilly

290 W Whitley   292 M Murray   294 J Bell   296 W Jordan

298 Mrs M Donoghue   300 J Caverley

442 J Goulding   444 J Mooney   446 J Browne

448 D Emmett   450 P Butterly

St Attracta Road

1 PJ Kelly   3 G Purdue   5 R Simpson   7 John Mc Cluskey

9 Maurice Behan   11 Charles Sweeney   13 P Ennis

15 James Flynn   17 John O' Connor   19 P Lawless

21 John Gillis   23 Joseph Kelly   25 John Kelly   27 C Dunne

29 J Mc Evoy   31 P Mc Kay   33 James Tobin   35 J Sweeney

37 John Mc Garry   39 William Keogh   41 P Byrne

43 Robert Clarkin   45 P Mc Hale   47 George Ramplin

49 J Lynch   51 Mrs P Mahon   53 William White

55 Mrs A Holmes   57 George Conway   59 Thomas Kerwin

61 Owen O' Hare

101 J Mc Evoy   103 V Beaver   105 P Whelan   107 P Meehan

109 M O' Reilly   111 John Allen   113 M Deegan

115 T Connor   117 P Finnegan   119 V Fallon   121 J Adams

123 Thomas Coates

St Attracta Road

265 M Ward   267 George Weir   269 Thomas Stephens

271 J Tyrrell   273 M Smart   275 C Farrell

277 A Mc Grath   279 M Dunne

2 Joseph Carolan   4 John Curren   6 William Lyons

8 DJ O'Neill   10 J O'Reilly   12 J Murray   14 S Benson

16 Thomas Mc Guinness   18 Joseph Mitchell   20 R Bassie

22 Richard O' Carroll   24 Michael Mc Creevy   26 M Kavanagh

28 John Whelan   30 Mrs Vesssy   32 J Farrell   34 F Carpenter

36 M Gaffney   38 M Mc Gouran   40 Mary Eastwood

90 P Boyle   92 P Hanlon   94 W G Ryan   96 P Maher

98 P Moore   100 Michael O' Connor   102 A Mc Evoy

104 M Lawless   106 R Dowling   108 Thomas Adams

110 J Hellier   112 M Keenan   114 Matthew Sheekey

116 Dennis Brown   118 M Beatty   120 P Curran

280   F Corney   282 W Tucker   284 J Kenny   286 J Ward

288 J Russell   290 W Conway   292 J Doran   294 J Brennan

296 Mrs O' Flaherty   298 S Mc Alorium   300 S Mc Cawley

Chapter 17

Places of Interest

Francis Street Market

Destruction of the Lord Gough Statue in the Phoenix Park 1957.

Nelson's Pillar destroyed in 1966

Williams & Woods Factory

'My first job was in Williams and Woods but I'll tell you about my job hunt. To show you how young I really was I was grown up at fourteen. It was in the summer and I'd left school. I decided I'd go and find a job and I wrote to Williams and Woods because a couple of my cousins worked there. My mam and dad were out one night so I wrote the letter and posted it. Then the next day I walked up to the Tin Box Factory in Ashtown. I walked in and asked for a job and they told me to come back next week or something, I can't remember but sometime later I got a letter from Williams and Woods asking me to go down for an interview. I went and started and that was it. Do you know something about Williams and Woods? Every now and again girls from the factory would be brought up to the office and had their hair combed for head lice'.

The Men's Labour Exchange in Gardiner Street

St Attracta Road

St Joseph's School on Rathoath Road

Hanlon's Corner

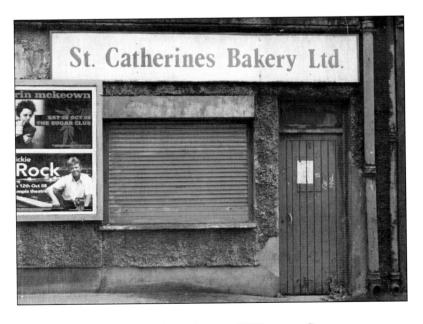

St Catherine's Bakery off Thomas Street

October 1951: *'The Dublin Board of Assistance today approved the recommendation of the visiting committee that a new dispensary be erected at Carnlough Road to serve the West Cabra housing area'.*

Moore Street Ladies

Animal Water Hole

Phibsboro' Statue

Accident on the River Liffey Dublin

Accidental Drowning

'On Tuesday 13th November 1951 the Evening Herald reported the death by drowning of two young English girls. A dense fog had enveloped most of Dublin City on that particular day. The two girls were returning by taxi to their guest house in Clontarf after spending an evening out. They had earlier dined in the Metropole Restaurant and later went dancing to the Four Provinces Ballroom in Harcourt Street. Two men crossing Butt Bridge reported hearing a loud splash in the river. On rushing to the quayside they saw a man struggling in the water. The man was rescued with the help of a life buoy. The taxi driver from Leix Road in Cabra was a non swimmer who managed to escape from his submerged taxi. The taxi had entered the water from the south side of the River Liffey'.

You Can't Go Home Again

Eugene Naughton

'Standing recently on the bridge at Fassaugh Avenue in Cabra, which spans the railway tracks and the heavenly hills of my childhood, I pondered Thomas Wolfe's great dictum: "You can't go home again". On the hills that were our mountains back then they have torn away the bushes and uprooted the trees that gave so much pleasure back in the days when we were never going to grow old. These are the hills, bushes and trees where we ambushed the Japanese and German armies and where we slaughtered General "Custard." They are building houses there now. More's the pity.
I lived in Cabra for all of my childhood and teens until I left home in my early twenties returning every now and then for visits and drinks with my father and brothers, birthday's and alas funeral's. Strolling past the vacated family home on my way over the bridge that morning I felt the long lost days of my youth pulling at me. I stopped and looked across to Jarleth Road and for some reason it seemed narrower now compared to the broad happy memories of my childhood. Nonetheless in the stillness of the cool morning air I could almost hear someone banging a can against the ground and a voice singing: "all in all in the game is broke up..."

Do children (never mind Cabra) these days still play those winter night games? 'Kick the Can.' 'Relievio'. 'Catch a Girl-Kiss a Girl'. Do they tell frightening ghost stories under street lamps like we used to?

And the summer holidays! Who among us then can ever forget the gloriously sunny days trekking to and from the Phoenix Park via the railway tracks? The bright long days spent on the hills behind our houses digging secret tunnels and roasting potatoes over wispy fires fueled by twigs and branches. Of course the same fires were used to send smoke signals to other warriors on the far side of the railway tracks who might be looking to do battle. And just in case my reminiscences seem too idyllic we weren't above stoning the passing trains that ran through our territory out of devilment and boredom. I don't know if we hurt anybody but we certainly scared the bejaysus out of them. And there was the swimming in the Royal Canal that ran above the railway tunnel at the back of the hills. We swam (usually naked) in a straight section of the canal that was known as the 'Bend' (so named because it was directly above the bend of the tunnel). As I write this I can still see 'Baldy' Prew taking a flying leap and jack-knifing into the air before breaking the water. None of us could match him for diving. Nobody swims there now I'm told. And then there was the lair, the playground, one for boys and one for girls. The playgrounds were a veritable paradise. The boy's playground contained everything from football pitches to handball alleys and the monkey puzzle. The girls also had a club-house and they too had swings, roundabouts, tennis courts, and areas for skipping and other games. Then there were the garden plots for growing vegetables, cultivated by both boys and girls. As we grew into our teens and twenties the playground was always there, particularly at night and on Sunday mornings when it was officially closed. Football and handball burned up the energies during the week and on Sunday mornings we played seven – a – side soccer matches for a 'dollar' (five shillings) a head, then afterwards into "Matts" for the first pint of the day. Cabra seems old to me now. Those dreamy hills are all fenced off now and the earth movers have moved in. 'Who's that I see coming through the gap? Why, it's General Custard; right into our trap'.

Conclusion

Old photographs and the stories behind them are priceless. A photograph represents a moment in time captured forever. The old Irish tradition of storytelling is still kept alive by many families today. Through the combination of these two methods of record keeping and with the assistance of modern day technology it is now possible to record the life and times of, not just individuals and their families but entire communities. Most every family had at least one photograph that was highly treasured and stored away for safe keeping. If there is any truth in the saying 'a picture paints a thousand words' then most family photographs will speak volumes. How often do we look at a photograph of our childhood and gain an instant recollection of the very moment the photograph was taken? This book is a testimony to the care and love that the owners of its photographs have shown over many years. These are their golden treasures. In some cases a photograph is all that is left of ones mother or father.

Now is the time to restore and recall all of those photographs and stories that we have been entrusted with from our parents and grandparents. Let us leave a legacy to future generations by combining our efforts together. The people of Cabra and Dublin have a great legacy to leave behind of the role that they and their families played in the history of our country. Now is the time to remember. If you would like to have your family's photographs and memories included in the next book of Cabra memories contact the author of this book by emailing to cabrahistory@yahoo.com. For more Cabra recollections visit the Cabra History.Com website.